Japan

Publishing Manager   Chris Milsome
Senior Editor   Chester Fisher
Editor   Dale Gunthorp
Design   Peter Benoist
Picture Research   Maggie Colbeck
Production   Philip Hughes
Illustrations   Ron Hayward Associates
  John Shackell
  Marilyn Day
  John Mousdale
  Tony Payne
Maps   Matthews and Taylor Associates
Special research   Syd Hoare
Consultant   Brian Hickman

Photographic sources Key to position of
illustrations: (T) top, (C) centre, (B)
bottom, (L) left, (R) right.
B.P.C. Picture Library 31(BR), 46(TL).
Camera Press 52(TR). Colin Craig 24(T),
29(BR). Mary Evans Picture Library
42(B). Joel Finler 13(TR). Syd and Sophy
Hoare 9(BR), 12(BL), 14(C), 15(TL),
17(TL), 19(TR), 20(B), 31(TL),
36(TL), 39(BC), 42(T), 43(BL), 43(BR),
49(TR). Imperial War Museum 46(B).
Japanese Embassy 44(TL), 44(BL),
45(TL), 53(B). Japanese Tourist Office
11(R), 16(T), 17(TR), 17(BL), 18(C),
19(TL), 21(TL), 22(T), 22(BC), 23(B),
24(B), 27(BR), 29(C), 30(T), 31(BL),
33(C), 33(B), 35(TL), 25(TR), 37(TL),
37(TR), 40(TL), 42(C), 47(BR),
52(TL). Mansell Collection 40(TR).
Janet March-Penney 32(B), 39(BR).
Pictor 9(TC), 15(C), 15(TL),
18(T), 23(T), 30(B), 37(BR), 38(C),
40(BL), 40(BC), 50(B). Productions
Television Recontre 9(TL), 8(BL),
8(TC), 8(BC), 13(TL), 31(TR), 35(BR),
47(BL). Radio Times Hulton Picture
Library 46(TC). Francis S   ner 9(TR),
   (B), 14(TL), 17(B), 17(BR), 20(TL),
21(B), 25(TL), 25(TR), 25(BL),
25(BR), 28(T), 29(L), 37(BL), 38(TL),
41(T), 47(T), 51(TC), 51(CR), 52(B).
Servizio Editoriale Fotografico 19(B),
33(T), 34(BC). Society for Educational
Information, Tokyo 18(BL). U.S. Navy
13(BL).

The **endpaper picture** shows Mount
Fuji, Japan's highest mountain. Fuji is a
dormant volcano, famous for its almost
perfect symmetry and snow-capped
summit.

First published 1975
Macdonald Educational Limited,
Holywell House
London, E. C. 2

© Macdonald Educational
Limited 1975

ISBN 0356 05100 5

Published in the United
States by Silver Burdett
Company, Morristown, N. J.
1976 Printing

Library of Congress
Catalog Card No. 75-44864

Page 6, Boys taking part in the *Tsuina*
("evil dispersing") festival held at the end
of winter. This 1,000 year old festival is
meant to ensure good luck. People shout
"in with good luck and out with the devil"
and scatter beans.

Japan

the land and its people

Sophy Hoare

Macdonald Educational

Contents

8 Ancient Japan

10 Land of contrasts

12 Japan's impact on the world

14 The family bond

16 Leisure time

18 Sport and the martial arts

20 The Japanese on holiday

22 Schools, and examinations

24 Shopping with style

26 Japanese cooking

28 Language and the media

30 Nature into art

32 Industry and crafts

34 Transport for a mobile nation

36 Customs and festivals

38 Buddhism and Shinto

40 Tokyo, the nerve-centre

42 The feudal era

44 The Meiji restoration

46 Hirohito: war and peace

48 Heroes of honour

50 The Japanese character

52 Facing the future

54 Reference: Geography and Government

56 Reference: History and the Arts

58 Reference: the Economy

60 Gazetteer

61 Index

62 Political map of Japan

63 Physical map of Japan

Ancient Japan

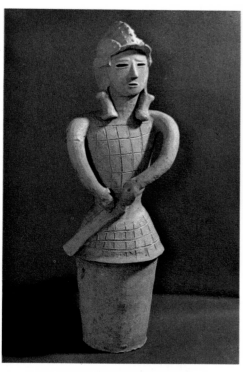

▼ A clay figure or "haniwa" of the fourth century A.D. These figures have been found on huge burial mounds containing the tombs of tribal chiefs.

▲ A scene from a twelfth century scroll which depicts the life of a courtier of the earlier Heian period. At that time (794–1185) Japan was ruled by the Fujiwara family. An elegant, courtly society grew up around the capital of Kyoto and the arts flourished.

Early settlers

The earliest Japanese were immigrants from the Asian continent, though when and how they arrived is not known. Today there are two racial types in Japan: the modern Japanese as we know them, with Mongoloid features like other north-east Asians, and a rapidly disappearing race, the Ainu.

Archaeologists have traced several cultures from about 8000 B.C. The first, the Jomon culture, left behind beautiful coiled earthenware pottery. Jomon people were nomads who ate nuts and shellfish and lived underground. From about 350 B.C. immigrants from China brought with them wheel-thrown pottery and objects made of bronze, stone and iron. They also cultivated rice. This period, the Yayoi, was succeeded by the Tomb culture which produced the earliest Japanese architecture.

Mythology to history

According to legend the Japanese empire was founded in 660 B.C. by Jimmu Tenno. He was a descendant of the god and goddess who created Japan.

In the fifth century A.D. a powerful clan in the Yamato area (around modern Kyoto) claimed to be descended from the divine Jimmu and established itself as the imperial family. The line is said to be unbroken to this day. There followed a long period of Chinese influence. This was encouraged at the turn of the sixth century by one of Japan's most remarkable rulers, Shotoku Taishi. By the ninth century the power of the imperial family had declined and the country was ruled by groups who acted in the emperor's name, a tradition which continued for a thousand years.

The feudal period in Japan lasted an unusually long time. From the tenth to the sixteenth centuries the country was often unsettled and ravaged by war. About two and a half centuries of peace under military rulers followed. They closed the country to contact with the outside world. It is only in 1854, with the reopening of her ports to foreign trade, that Japan's modern history begins.

▲ An early wall painting of a Buddha, showing Indian influence. It is in one of the oldest wooden buildings in the world, Horyuji temple at Nara. Buddhism was introduced to Japan in the sixth century A.D.

This thirteenth century painting shows a scene from the Heiji Monogatari, or Tales of the Heiji War. This war marked the end of Fujiwara rule in 1159—60 and the seizing of power by the Taira family. It was one of many military revolutions in Japan.

▲ The majority of Japanese are of Mongolian type, with flattish faces, high cheekbones and almond-shaped eyes with fatty eyelids. The skin is an even brownish colour and hair is coarse and black.

▼ A "hairy Ainu". There are very few Ainu people left in Japan. They may be a Caucasian race, like Europeans and Indians. Unlike the rest of the Japanese, they have abundant facial and body hair.

Land of contrasts

Tradition and change

Japan is a land of great contrasts. That between old and new pervades its life. Japan's long isolation policy was followed by sudden contact with Western culture in the nineteenth century; and Japan is both eager to adopt new ideas and reluctant to do away with old traditions. Today, seemingly incongruous elements of Eastern and Western culture exist side by side.

Japan is also a land of natural contrasts. The traveller crossing Japan finds crowded plains as well as untouched mountain scenery broken here and there by clusters of thatched farm buildings and small neat rice fields.

The same traveller notices an unusual range of climate for a country of Japan's size. The islands extend 3,000 kilometres from north to south and are exposed to different air currents. Heavy snows fall in the north and tropical plants grow in the south. In June it rains every day, but at other times of the year it is very sunny.

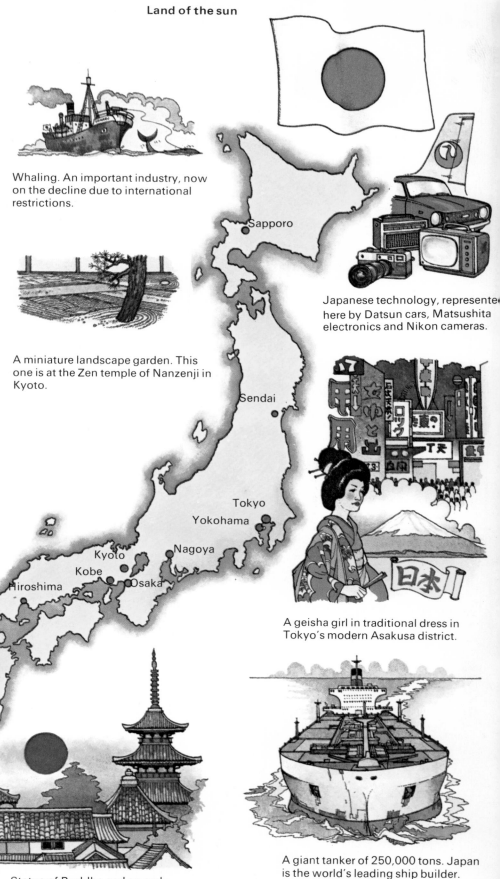

Whaling. An important industry, now on the decline due to international restrictions.

A miniature landscape garden. This one is at the Zen temple of Nanzenji in Kyoto.

Japanese technology, represente[d] here by Datsun cars, Matsushita electronics and Nikon cameras.

The battle of Tsushima. Japan, a new world power, destroyed the Russian fleet in two days.

A geisha girl in traditional dress in Tokyo's modern Asakusa district.

Statue of Buddha and an early Buddhist temple at Nara. There are many Buddhist sects.

A giant tanker of 250,000 tons. Japan is the world's leading ship builder.

▲ Japan has great natural beauty. Most of the land is mountainous and covered in forest, providing two most important resources: wood and hydro-electric power.

◄ Much of Japan's coastline is still unspoilt. The sea has always been the chief source of protein and today Japan catches and eats more fish than any other country, except Peru.

▼ Rush hour on a Tokyo station. In contrast to the remote mountains, Japan's plains are among the most densely populated regions in the world. About 70 per cent of the people live in cities, and of these 58 per cent are in four metropolitan areas.

Japan's impact on the world

▼ The Japanese tourist has become a common sight abroad. Industrial wealth, and curiosity about foreign techniques, have led to the invasion of other countries by Japanese businessmen. They usually travel in groups and are always armed with cameras. Close study of foreign manufacturing methods has enabled the Japan to produce high quality goods at very competitive prices.

▲ Judo originated in Japan and is now an Olympic sport practised all over the world. Judo means "the gentle or pliant way". This implies using one's opponent's movement to one's own advantage rather than resisting it. The end result is not always gentle!

Japanese Business

Under the constitution enforced after the Second World War, Japan was forbidden to retain her army, and so she worked at becoming a leading industrial nation. Although she now has a self-defence force, only a small fraction of the budget is spent on defence. Perhaps Japan's biggest influence on the world today is from her invasion of world markets. Her products range from tankers to musical instruments. Her growth rate in industrial production in the last decade far exceeded that of even the Soviet Union and West Germany. Japanese industries were so successful in selling products abroad that other countries became worried about keeping level with Japanese competition. They feared an imbalance in world trade, and in 1971 America introduced the first of her anti-Japan economic measures by putting a tax surcharge on Japanese imports.

The Second World War

During the period just before the War Japan had been steadily extending her empire, with the colonization of Korea and Manchuria. Her surprise attack on the American fleet in Pearl Harbour in 1941 caused a European war to become a World War. The Japanese advanced rapidly early in the War. They captured Singap from the British in 1942, and soon gai control of Burma, the Philippines, T land, Vietnam, most of Indonesia, H Kong and the Pacific almost as far Hawaii. Japan was finally defeated by o whelming American and Allied forces, only after fighting to the bitter end.

Even in defeat Japan has impressed world, showing her ability to rise from r fortune and begin again. After the W under American occupation, the Japan very quickly directed their energies i creating a prosperous and peaceful sta Japan is the only country to have been by the atomic bomb, yet Hiroshima, chief target, is today a flourishing city. charred shell of a building which mirac ously withstood the attack stands as a minder to the world of the horror of nucl destruction.

In other ways, Japan remains somew apart from the rest of the world. Her rem geographical position and the difficul of the language make communication di cult. Few foreigners speak Japanese and Japanese themselves show no great tal for languages. Although Japan's influen in the arts has been considerable, it co be much greater, for Japan has a ri cultural tradition.

▲ A painting by Suzuki Harunobu, an eighteenth century artist. Harunobu was also one of the first artists to produce the coloured wood-block prints which later inspired the French Impressionist painters in the nineteenth century.

▼ A scene from the film *The Seven Samurai* by the great director, Kurosawa. This is his best known film and it inspired the western, *The Magnificent Seven*. Kurosawa is one of many Japanese film directors who have influenced world cinema.

▼ Attack on Pearl Harbour, Hawaii, in 1941. This brilliant piece of daring crippled the American navy in one blow, enabling the Japanese to make conquests in South-East Asia. But it didn't help in the long run, since it caused America to declare war.

▲ A Japanese factory abroad. The Japanese have set up many factories overseas, especially in other Asian countries such as Thailand and Korea. In a crisis, the managers would not hesitate to roll up their sleeves to help out.

The family bond

▲ There are many apartment blocks like this one in Japanese towns. The flats are small and partitions between them are often thin, so residents are usually well acquainted with their neighbours! Outside the towns, most people still live in the traditional house of wood.

◄ The Japanese do not have separate bedrooms but use the same rooms for living and sleeping. Bedding is stored in cupboards during the day and spread out on the floor at night. A bed consists of two mattress pads underneath and a thick quilt on top, and is extremely cosy.

The atmosphere of intimacy

The Japanese have a more communal way of living than most Western countries. Individual privacy is not highly valued and members of a family are brought up in an atmosphere of intimacy from the moment they are born. A baby is carried strapped to its mother's back and travels everywhere with her. A family of five may live in two or three small rooms divided by sliding paper doors.

The traditional house is made of wood and built to a pattern which dates back to the fifteenth century. It is built to withstand the hot summers rather than the cold winters. Common features are an entrance porch, an alcove in the living room, sliding doors, and straw mats or "tatami" on the floor. The tatami determine the dimensions of a room. A standard tatami mat is 1·8 metres × 0·9 metres (6 ft × 3 ft) and room sizes are given in mats: a six mat room, a four and a half mat room, and so on.

The tatami are about eight centimetres (three inches) thick and filled with straw. They are kept scrupulously clean since the family sits on them by day and sleeps on them at night. Outdoor shoes are left at the front door. Slippers are worn on the wooden floors of the passages and socks or bare feet on the tatami.

However, with the building of apartment blocks in the cities, the pattern of homes is gradually changing. New flats, though small by Western standards, often have central heating and air conditioning and offer some protection against fire.

A day in the life of a Japanese family

7.30 Breakfast time

8.30 At school

8.30 Father at work

6.30 Mother makes breakfast

2.00 Back to lessons, or gym

2.00 Father busy at work

2.00 Mother does the cleaning

4.30 School is over for the day

◄ Mixed bathing in a country district. Every neighbourhood has its public bath house, so few families have a bathroom at home. Bathing is almost a ritual—most people bathe once or twice a day—and it is just as much a form of relaxation and social contact as a way of getting clean. The bath house has several pools of clean water at temperatures ranging from hot to scalding. These are for soaking in after one has washed oneself at the taps in the surrounding area.

▼ A family sits down to a meal, surrounded by its possessions. Electrical gadgets are beginning to fill people's homes, but most families keep at least one room free of clutter and furnished in the sparse traditional style.

▲ A father and son playing *pachinko* or pinball. Family ties are very close, and family members feel a sense of duty to each other, especially to the older generation. There is also a strong sense of security.

.00 Mother goes shopping

12.30 School lunch

12.30 Father lunches at the canteen

12.30 Grandmother, mother and baby have lunch at home

6.45 Family bathtime

7.30 Supper

11.00 Bedtime for everybody

Leisure time

Geisha houses and coffee bars

Japanese cities have much to offer in the way of entertainment. There are traditional geisha houses, music halls and sumo wrestling matches, and modern bars and night clubs. Coffee bars are a favourite meeting ground for young people. The price of coffee is rather high, but it includes really good service, with a glass of iced water offered on arrival, and a damp hand towel, steaming hot in winter and refreshingly cold in summer. Many coffee houses specialize in playing classical music or jazz on high quality equipment, and people go to listen rather than to talk.

Today of course the mass media play a large part in occupying people's leisure.

Television is the most common form of entertainment at home, and a huge output of newspapers and magazines provides plenty of reading matter.

Mountains and beaches

When they have time, the Japanese love to escape from the strain of city life. Probably the most popular way of spending a day off is to take a train out of town to the country or the sea. During the summer Tokyo's beaches become as crowded as its underground in the rush hour. Hiking in the mountains is a favourite way of relaxing and may be combined with a stay in one of Japan's many hot spring resorts.

The Japanese are a very gregarious people and tend to do most things in groups but they seldom join independent clubs and societies. Firms usually provide leisure facilities for their employees and even send them to holiday resorts for a short escape from the strains of working life.

The Japanese are very often most accomplished people, and if they take up a hobby they devote as much serious study to it as to their work. There is little of the amateur in them and they are prepared to spend years acquiring a skill such as calligraphy, dancing, or playing a musical instrument.

▲ One of Tokyo's many night clubs. Tokyo very lively at night, with clubs to suit every taste and every pocket.

▼ Appreciating the cherry blossom in spring is an annual rite and many people take picnics to the parks and countryside.

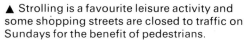
▲ Strolling is a favourite leisure activity and some shopping streets are closed to traffic on Sundays for the benefit of pedestrians.

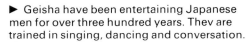
▶ Geisha have been entertaining Japanese men for over three hundred years. They are trained in singing, dancing and conversation.

A class studying the art of flower arrangement. Japanese spend much of their leisure time learning new skills. Classes are especially popular with women.

Golf is one of the most popular sports. It is expensive to join a club, but many people are able to enjoy facilities provided by their firm.

Sport and the martial arts

Olympic stars

The Japanese are keen sports players, and their capacity for diligent, conscientious practice has won them international success not only in their traditional sports such as judo, but also in gymnastics, swimming, volleyball, weightlifting and wrestling. In the 1972 Olympics the Japanese dominated the men's gymnastics events, with one man, Kato, winning three gold medals. Their small swimming team won two gold medals and a bronze.

The two national sports, which have as many enthusiastic supporters as football has in Europe, are sumo wrestling and baseball. Sumo is the oldest sport in Japan. The first national tournament was held in 728 A.D., but the sport dates back well before that, and was a popular entertainment at festivals and shrines. The ancient rules and etiquette give sumo its appeal as a spectacle.

Apart from the Japanese martial arts, which are still widely practised and are taught in schools, the most popular sports are probably skiing and golf. Golf was introduced to Japan in 1903 by a Japanese who had learned to play at Greenwich Naval College. He founded the first golf club at Kobe. During the 1950s the sport suddenly became popular. Today there are over 700 golf courses.

▲ A sumo wrestling match is a combination of physical power, showmanship and skill. The average weight of a wrestler is around 20 stone. The wrestlers perform a lengthy and symbolic ritual before the contest. The action is usually over in seconds. The contest is decided when one wrestler is pushed or dropped out of the ring or brought to the ground. The only part of the body allowed to touch the ground is the sole of the foot. The technique is complicated, with over 70 *waza*, or moves. Sumo is a highly professional sport. The top rank in Japan is known as *Yokozuna*, or Grand Champion.

◄ Baseball was introduced to Japan from America in 1874 and is now firmly established as a national sport, with a system of professional leagues and university teams. The yearly match between the Tokyo universities of Keio and Waseda is an event comparable to America's Army and Navy football game.

◄ Japanese archery is very different from western archery. The bow is asymmetrical and the bowstring is drawn well past the ear, until both arms are outstretched. Like the other martial arts, such as judo, karate, and kendo, Japanese archery is highly ritualized and is a training for mental as well as physical control. The aim is not only to hit the bull's eye on the target but also to develop a particular form of self discipline.

▼ Kendo—bamboo sword fighting—is a sport based on the old sword fighting methods of the *samurai*, the warriors of the feudal age. When practising their fighting technique, the *samurai* substituted bamboo sticks for their long swords. Today Kendo is one of the more popular martial arts and, like judo, is taught in schools from an early age. The contestants wear armour and score points by hitting specific parts of their opponent's body. Like the other martial arts, Kendo training includes meditation and rigorous training sessions at the coldest and hottest times of the year.

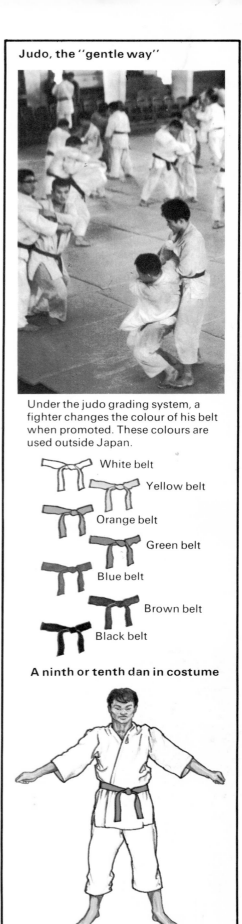

Judo, the "gentle way"

Under the judo grading system, a fighter changes the colour of his belt when promoted. These colours are used outside Japan.

White belt
Yellow belt
Orange belt
Green belt
Blue belt
Brown belt
Black belt

A ninth or tenth dan in costume

The Japanese on holiday

▲ People setting off on holiday usually travel by public transport, and they travel light, since holidays are often only two or three days long.

Getting away for a few days

Holidays in Japan are usually short and often taken with a group of friends. People do visit relatives in distant parts of the country, but the long family holiday away from home is rare. There are many mountain and hot-spring resorts, and beauty spots. The hotels range from cheap hostels for hikers to luxurious traditional inns with huge hot baths run directly from the volcanic spring water. Most trips are for two or three days only.

Japan has a wide range of climate, and much of the land is mountainous with some beautiful scenery. Winter sports are popular, and the Japanese are enthusiastic sightseers. Tourism within the country is well organized: posters advertising different regions of Japan are displayed at every station. Much is made of regional specialities and it is a custom, almost an obligation, for holiday-makers to bring back samples of local produce for friends and neighbours.

The popular choice for holidays abroad is Hawaii, but more and more people travel as far as America, and even Europe.

Traditional inns

One of the chief pleasures of travelling in Japan, is to stay in traditional inns or *ryokan*. These are very clean and comfortable. The service is delightfully hospitable. On arriving, the traveller is greeted with a pair of slippers and a pot of tea waiting in the room; then given a freshly laundered kimono to change into, and directed to the hot bath for a leisurely soak. Meanwhile the beds are laid out and dinner prepared. The meal is served in one's own room. This procedure is always the same. It is reassuring for weary travellers to know in advance that they will spend a comfortable night.

Japan has much to offer the foreign tourist. Perhaps the place which attracts most foreigners is Kyoto, the ancient capital and centre of the arts. Unlike Tokyo, Kyoto was not damaged during the War, and has over 2,000 temples and shrines.

Festive holidays in Japan

The Japanese have a number of colourful festivals, with their own special ceremonial.

▲ Holiday makers strolling in the temple grounds at Nara. A favourite way of spending holidays is to make pilgrimages to monuments and shrines. In the old days these tours were done on foot and took weeks at a time. Today's pilgrims are whisked around by coach.

◄ Although holidays are short, there are many annual festivals held in different regions of Japan. These are usually colourful occasions when people enjoy dressing in traditional costume, preparing special food and flying kites and paper streamers. Festivals may be held in honour of local shrines, ancestors, children and even dolls.

◄ Winter sports are becoming more and more popular. Since mountain ranges cover the whole of Japan, there are always snow and ice to be found within reach of home.

▼ A guest arrives at a traditional inn. The entire hotel staff may appear on the threshold to welcome his arrival, offer little comforts, and to wish him a safe journey when he leaves.

The national holidays

January 1	New Year's Day
January 15	Adults' Day
February 11	Commemoration of the Founding of the Nation
March 21	Vernal Equinox Day
April 29	Emperor's Birthday
May 3	Constitution Day
May 5	Children's Day
September 15	Respect for the Aged
September 24	Autumnal Equinox
October 10	Health-Sports Day
November 3	Culture Day
November 23	Labour Thanksgiving

◄ There are a number of yearly national holidays which originated as religious festivals but which today are little more than secular bank holidays.

▼ One of the many beautiful beaches that are found along Japan's extensive coastline. Everyone lives within reach of the sea as the islands form a crescent shape.

21

Schools and examinations

▶ Children at primary school. The educational level of the Japanese has always been high, with much importance attached to teaching the very young. Although compulsory education begins at the age of six years, there are many kindergarten schools.

The Japanese school system

Technical college 15-20

Junior college 18-20 years

Postgraduate study, over 21

Elementary school 6-12 years

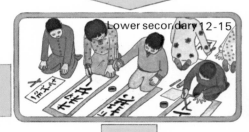

Lower secondary 12-15

Upper secondary 15-18

University 18-21 years

▲ The present educational system is modelled on the American and European systems. Education is compulsory for nine years and state schools are free. There are also many private institutions.

Universal education

Japan's educational system has undergone two major reforms in recent history. The first of these, in the 1870s, was the creation of a new system of universal education by the recently formed Ministry of Education. In the early twentieth century almost all children attended schools, and six years at elementary school were compulsory. This system gave equal chances to children from different classes of society, though only the most able pupils reached high school and university.

However, the system was also highly centralized, and by the Second World War it had become a tool in the hands of the government to shape the kind of citizen most useful to its aims. Obedience and patriotism were instilled into the young Japanese with militaristic and anti-Western propaganda.

The post-war schools

The second reform came when the American occupation authorities replaced the old text books and introduced comprehensive schools.

With freer access to higher education, university standards were generally lowered, but opportunities were of course far

...ider. Today there is a great number of universities, many of them private. There are dozens in Tokyo alone. There is no streaming by ability within schools, and classes are large. One interesting method of learning is that the more advanced pupils help others who have difficulty with the lessons. However, the standard of schools and universities varies considerably, and competition to get into a good one is quite fierce.

From the moment they go to school, Japanese students face a rigorous course of examinations. Entrance exams determine their placing at university and again their employment, which will probably be with the same company for life. The pressure of exams is a heavy burden for students especially for boys. Even today, girls are not encouraged to take up a career, and devote more study to skills like *ikebana*.

The final year at high school is known as the "exam hell". Having entered a university of their choice, students can relax until the fourth year; then they take the company entrance exams. Once they are safely employed by a reputable company, the competition eases off, since promotion is granted with age, and it is almost impossible to be dismissed.

◀ A class at secondary school. Japanese schools are well equipped with modern teaching aids and academic standards are high, especially in mathematics. The traditional approach to education is one of learning by rote and Japanese children are required to absorb a large number of facts. But gradually more emphasis is being placed on teaching students to think for themselves.

▲ High school girls on an outing, wearing the national navy-blue uniform.

▼ The number of students at universities and colleges has doubled over the past ten years. Apart from early childhood, the university years are probably the most carefree in the life of a Japanese. Exams and social pressures to conform are forgotten for a while.

Shopping with style

Traditional shops and markets

The small neighbourhood shop still thrives in Japan. These little shops have a cotton curtain or *noren* hanging at the entrance which displays the name and trademark of the shop. The Japanese give much importance to efficient and polite service, which probably explains the lack of supermarkets.

Food is the biggest expenditure in the family budget, and fresh food is often bought at the local covered market. Meat is expensive and so are Western forms of food such as butter, cheese, milk and bread. Rice, still the staple food, is sold only at special shops. Vegetables and fruit are of good quality, and greengrocers display their wares with artistry.

Grand department stores

For people who want to buy everything under one roof there are big department stores in every large town. These have sections for clothes, and household goods, and there is usually one floor devoted to traditional costume with all its accessories, and a wide range of silk fabrics. There is generally a huge food department selling cooked delicacies as well as basic foodstuffs. Although these stores are often very large, the customer receives the same personal service as in the small shops. Foreign visitors are somewhat surprised to see the uniformed women standing at the foot of the escalators, with the sole function of welcoming the customers, wiping the handrail and bowing politely to them as they step on!

There are fewer packaged foods than in the West and plastic carrier bags are seldom seen. The Japanese are experts at wrapping, and still use bamboo sheaths for wrapping fresh food such as meat. The traditional way of carrying shopping is in a *furoshiki*: that is, a square cloth made of silk or cotton, often of beautiful design. The shopping or parcel is placed in the centre and the four corners are brought together and tied.

When the shopping is done, the shopkeeper will probably add up the bill on an electronic calculator, then check the result on his *soroban*, the traditional Japanese abacus!

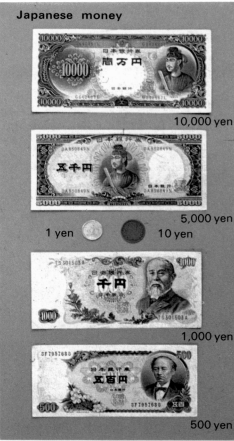

Japanese money

10,000 yen

5,000 yen

1 yen   10 yen

1,000 yen

500 yen

▲ Japanese currency is based on the yen: 100 yen is worth roughly 15p. A cup of coffee might cost 120 yen, a family car 500,000 yen.

▼ Department stores are a marvellous mixture of east and west. They sell a huge range of goods, from cheap souvenirs and cut-price clothing to precious jewels and antiques.

Monthly Income 112,000 yen

34,900 yen Education, transport and recreation

An average family's monthly budget

26,600 yen Food

21,000 yen Savings and pensions

9,300 yen Housing

9,300 yen Insurance etc

8,800 yen Clothes

3,000 yen Fuel

24

▲ The decorations at the entrance of this building mark the opening of a new shop. This event is accompanied by a traditional ceremony. The ceremony is normally presided over by the local Shinto priest. This is one of many commonplace Japanese customs bound up with the beliefs of the Shinto religion.

◄▲ Most day-to-day shopping is done at the small local shops or street markets. Japanese housewives prefer to buy their food fresh every day rather than to stock up for the week. There are shops for every type of household product. In one street one might find separate shops selling tatami (straw mats), lanterns, umbrellas, quilts, hand painted signs and various kinds of pickles, grains and dried beans. The beans are sold loose from large sacks or barrels. In the craft shops you can often watch the shopkeeper making his products, seated in traditional style on the floor. Paper lanterns as well as signs display the names of shops and restaurants.

► Every neighbourhood has its market. There are many covered food markets which sell a wide variety of traditional food. At some stalls one can buy fresh oysters, prawns and other fish and vegetables dipped in batter and fried on the spot to take away. There are also regular markets which sell everything from clothes, books and antiques to dried snakes for medicinal purposes.

Japanese cooking

Menu for a typical day

▼ Typical meals for a day. The breakfast is traditional, although many people now eat eggs, toast and coffee in the morning. The cold lunch would be served in summer and the evening stew is a typical winter meal.

Breakfast : clear miso (bean curd) soup, rice, raw or fried egg, pickles, green tea.

Lunch : cold noodles, pickled vegetables, soya sauce, green tea.

Supper : stew of meat or seafood with bean curd and vegetables. Rice. Satsumas and persimmons.

Rice and raw fish

In Japanese the word for food and the word for rice are the same. Not only is rice eaten at every meal, but it is often served on its own, garnished with a few pickled vegetables or pieces of dried fish. Its quality is savoured, much as wines are in the West. There is a great variety of sea food and vegetables and almost as many ways of preparing them.

The Japanese have never been great meat eaters, mainly because there is a shortage of grazing land, and partly because Buddhism prohibits the slaughter of animals. Today, however, meat and dairy products are becoming more widely available. All the larger towns have at least one butcher. One of the chief sources of protein is the soya bean, which is cheap and nourishing. It is used as a paste to make a basis for soups, and as a solid curd which can be fried or put into stews.

There is a saying that the Japanese eat with their eyes. The appearance of a meal is as important as its taste, which is very delicate. People eat out frequently; and as well as the noodle shops and *sushi* bars found in every other street there are many Chinese and Korean restaurants, and places which serve pork chops and spaghetti as well as Japanese food.

Although the Japanese normally eat with chopsticks, and can even handle a fried egg with them, knives and forks are now commonly found in restaurants. Water or tea are usually drunk with meals. Tea, nearly always green, is taken without sugar or milk. The chief alcoholic drinks are sake, a kind of wine distilled from rice, and Japanese beer.

Make yourself a Japanese meal

Ingredients for Sukiyaki
1 lb **tender steak**, sliced like bacon
1 tin **shirataki** (thin noodles) drained
1 tin **bamboo shoots**
1 lb **small leeks** (or spring onions)
½lb **mushrooms**
2 cakes **tofu** (soya bean curd)
Bunch of chrysanthemum leaves (or watercress)
small piece of beef fat
¼ **pint Japanese soya sauce**
2-3 oz **sugar**
3-9 tablespoons **sake** (optional)
4 **eggs**

Slice the vegetables and bean curd and arrange with the meat on a large dish. In Japan, sukiyaki is cooked on a gas ring placed in the middle of a low table. But you can cook it on an ordinary stove in batches. The food should be eaten as soon as it is cooked. Melt the beef fat in a heavy flat frying pan. Add some of the meat and leeks or onions, allow to brown a little, then pour in a little water with sugar dissolved in it, and sprinkle with soy sauce and sake. Once the juices from the meat have mixed with the cooking liquid, add more meat and vegetables. Take out the pieces of food when cooked, and serve.

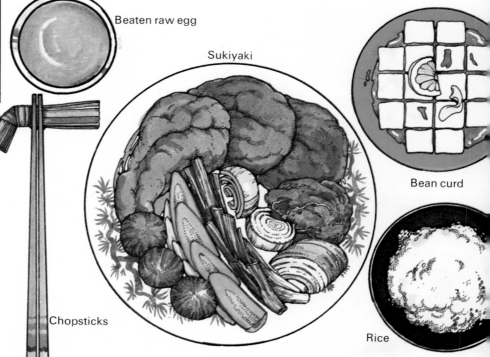

Beaten raw egg

Sukiyaki

Bean curd

Chopsticks

Rice

Sashimi : Sliced raw fish served with various spicy dipping sauces and garnished with grated radish. The fish is absolutely fresh and is cut by a special method to give even slices or cubes. The most popular fish are squid, tunny, sea bream and bass.

▼ **Tempura :** Food coated in a light batter and deep fried. It usually consists of fish, especially prawns or oysters, and vegetables such as aubergine, sweet potato, green pepper and chrysanthemum leaves. Tempura is eaten with a dipping sauce.

▼ **Kyogashi :** The Japanese do not eat a dessert at mealtimes, but they have a variety of sweets often eaten on special occasions such as birthdays and weddings. These confections are very sweet and decoratively coloured and packed.

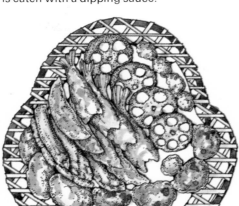

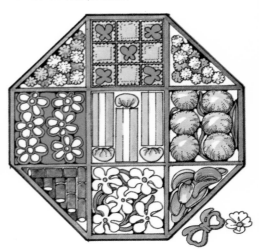

To eat :
Each person should be provided with a bowl of boiled rice, another small bowl, a raw egg and a pair of chopsticks. Break the egg into the bowl and beat it lightly with the chopsticks. When the food is served, dip the cooked meat and vegetables into the egg and eat it, taking mouthfuls of rice in between. If you have a piece of meat which is too large to eat in one go, it is quite good manners to hold it in the chopsticks and bite pieces off. Sake is usually drunk with sukiyaki (from egg-cup sized bowls), but beer or tea go with it very well.

Soy sauce

Salad

◀ A *bento*, or picnic box. These beautifully prepared wooden boxes usually contain rice in one compartment and fish and vegetables in the other. They come complete with chopsticks and a miniature bottle of soy sauce. They are usually eaten while travelling and are sold on trains and at stations. *Bento* often include some local speciality.

▼ A family meal. The Japanese do not normally serve separate courses but lay the complete meal on the table in individual bowls with lids to keep the food hot. They have a gift for making a meal look beautiful. Even a bowl of clear soup is garnished with freshly sliced vegetables in a contrasting colour.

Language and media

The Japanese script, with two alphabets

あしたの天気

These characters mean:

Tomorrow's weather

The first four characters are phonetic symbols from the Japanese alphabet, meaning "TOMORROW'S"

The last two are pictorial symbols, representing the word "WEATHER"

▲ Election poster backing a communist candidate. Calligraphy and the picture form a whole.

◄ Japanese is usually written from top to bottom and then from right to left. Calligraphy is an art form as well as a means of communication. Done properly, it is written with a brush and black Indian ink on rice paper. There can be no "drawing up" and no rubbing out. The rice paper absorbs the ink like blotting paper and it requires a delicate but sure touch to obtain the right balance of strokes. Calligraphy can form part of a work of art. Painting and wood block prints are often adorned by poems and signatures.

The Japanese language

The Japanese adopted the Chinese script many centuries ago. This script uses ideographs, or pictures, to express ideas; not symbols to stand for sounds. Some ideographs look like the objects they represent, such as the character for "man", which is 人, and for "mouth", which is 口. They are not always so obvious: they have evolved and been stylized over thousands of years. But, although Japanese is written in the Chinese script, it is quite a different sort of language from Chinese in other ways. A Japanese and a Chinese translate the same ideograph into two different words, and wouldn't understand each other, though they could sketch the ideographs on each other's palm, and so make some communication. Chinese characters could not be adapted to express Japanese ideas, so the Japanese invented two 48-letter phonetic scripts to be used with them. Thus a Japanese child has to learn about 2,000 characters and two 48-letter alphabets to be literate.

Calligraphy and printing

Although the Japanese have invented a typewriter for their script, it is a cumbersome apparatus, and handwritten notices are quite acceptable for business and other official communications. The typewriter is reserved for very formal occasions. In fact, a message written by a skilled calligrapher looks just as official as a typewritten one. The legal method of identification in Japan is not by signature, but by personal seal.

Despite the difficulties of the written language, the Japanese have always been voracious readers. There was a big increase in publications at the end of the War, and today Japan has over a hundred daily papers. Japanese papers have the largest circulation in the world after the United States.

Broadcasting

Japan has a complex system of communication across the country. There are many radio stations and television channels, though the programmes are often poor. Japan was the second country in the world to start regular colour television broadcasting. There are T.V. sets in 84 per cent of homes and sometimes it seems difficult to escape from the "telly" or *terebi* as they call it in Japan. Television sets are often installed in bars and coffee houses, and even in trains and buses.

Japanese television

ere are numerous commercial television annels as well as the national broadcasting rporation, NHK. Television starts at six in e morning and goes on all day, so it is not rprising that the standard of programmes is t consistently high.

The main body of entertainment on the commercial channels consists of variety shows, quiz programmes, horror movies, comedy series, chat programmes, children's cartoons, "monster" films and imported dubbed westerns. There are also a great many *samurai* films. The tradition of *samurai* films is somewhat like that of the American western. Like the western, there are a number of classic *samurai* films, called "chambara", which means "the clash of swords". However a great many more mediocre ones are produced.

NHK tends to broadcast more documentaries, news programmes, serious music and educational programmes. There is a news and weather report every hour. A typical day's broadcasting would be as follows:

6-8 News, weather, exercises, farming report.
8.30-11 Programmes for housewives such as fashion, cookery, calligraphy or flower arranging, care of old people. Programmes for young children.
12-1 Light entertainment and news.
2-3 More domestic programmes and more exercises.
3.30-5 Music, such as Puccini's *Madame Butterfly*
5-7 Light entertainment, and perhaps a thriller.
7.30-8.30 Local news, documentary.
8.30-9.30 Film or variety show.
9.30-11 Historical programme, news in depth, foreign film.
11 News and sport.
11.15 Close down.

◄ The pressure of advertising is as insistent in Japan as in any Western capitalist country. Neon lights hang side by side with traditional signs, advertisements leap at you from magazines and from posters on public transport. Key words and phrases are frequently written in Roman letters. In fact the streets in Japanese cities display a jumble of cultures.

Japanese cinema. Japan produces and ws more films than any other country. ough a large proportion of the films wn are made in Japan, successful ppean and American films reach Tokyo in a week or two of their release. The anese are such experts at dubbing that ny Japanese children are under the impres- that the whole world speaks Japanese!

he average Japanese household takes daily papers. The biggest national dailies the *Asahi*, the *Mainichi* and the *Yomiuri*. re are also several newspapers in English, h as the *Japan Times*. The bottom row of gazines in this picture shows a few of the y weekly publications, including a film gazine.

Nature into art

The influence of Zen

In spite of much early borrowing from China, Japan has a very individual aesthetic tradition. The Japanese have a number of untranslatable words which describe their concept of beauty. One example is the word *sabi* which literally means loneliness, and conveys a pleasurable sense of the old, the faded, the slightly melancholy. The fallen flower and the withered branch are as beautiful as the tree in full blossom. This quality is present in much of their literature and can be glimpsed in this translation of a poem by the seventeenth century poet, Basho:

> *A crow is perched*
> *Upon a leafless withered bough—*
> *The autumn dusk.*

Zen Buddhism has contributed towards this preference for economy of expression. Typical Zen art forms are the raked garden of carefully chosen rocks in a sea of raked white sand, and the impressionistic landscape painting perfected by the fifteenth century artist, Sesshu.

Fusing art and nature

The Japanese art of fusing art and nature is seen clearly in the architecture. For practical as well as aesthetic reasons in a land of forests and earthquakes, wood is the traditional building material. It is generally left unpainted. The garden is landscaped in harmony with the interior. Massive structures and perfect symmetry are usually avoided, and buildings are conceived on a human scale. These general principles have continued to apply to present-day domestic architecture.

The spectacular side of Japanese popular art is typified by the *Kabuki* theatre, a type of drama which originated in the sixteenth century and contrasts strongly with the famous *Noh* theatre. The plays contain much action and are often highly sentimental in theme. The stage sets are extraordinarily elaborate and realistic. Female roles are played by men, a convention which Japanese actors have developed into a high dramatic art.

▲ A wood block print, *The Waves* by the great landscape artist, Hokusai (1760-1849). Wood block printing was first used to illustrate Buddhist scriptures and later to produce cheap, popular prints and illustrations for books.

◄ A scene from Kurosawa's film, *Yojimbo*, about a *samurai* who is hired to help settle a feud in a small country town. "Yojimbo" means a hired hand or bodyguard. After making deals with both sides, Yojimbo allows them to destroy each other. Japanese films have won many awards at international film festivals.

▼ One of the most famous Japanese art forms is the *Noh* drama, over six hundred years old. It has changed little since the sixteenth century, when the great dramatist Zeami wrote a treatise on its artistic principles. *Noh* is a stylised drama performed as slow dance or mime to the accompaniment of music. The stage is almost bare, the only set being a backcloth depicting a pine tree. The actors wear masks and elaborate costumes and their movements are stylized. *Noh* is very symbolic and the drama lies in the slow build up to an emotional climax.

▲ An early Buddhist sculpture in bronze. The arts closely associated with Buddhism were among the first borrowings from China. By the eighth century Japanese artists had mastered the foreign techniques and styles.

A musician playing the *koto*, a 13-stringed instrument resembling the zither. It is one of the instruments used to play *Gagaku*, a type of courtly music which came to Japan from China in the eighth century and which is played in the same form today.

Daigoji temple at Kyoto is a typical example of early Japanese Buddhist architecture, with its deep roofs and towering pagoda. It shows a direct Chinese influence and is very different from the early native Japanese architecture with thatched roofs.

Industry and crafts

Arranging marriages

Holidays at company lodge

Pensions

Housing

Medical services

Newcomers to industry

Japan is one of the leading industrial nations of the world, yet fairly recently she was almost completely cut off from foreign trade, with a rural society bound by ancient conventions. When contact with other countries was renewed in the middle of the nineteenth century, the Government began an ambitious industrialization programme, borrowing and adapting techniques from the West. Close links between big business and the Government have remained.

After defeat in the Second World War, and American occupation, Japan started a fresh climb toward prosperity, with American aid. She began to export a wide range of manufactured goods and gained a reputation for high quality products, especially cameras, electronics and precision instruments.

Heavy and advanced technological industry grew in importance and Japan began to transfer lighter industries to other Asian countries where labour was cheap. After years of experience and careful refinement of foreign techniques, Japan is now beginning to export her own expertise to other countries. Japan's steel technology is unsurpassed.

Japan, having few natural resources, imports raw materials and fuel. Her large iron and steel industry, for instance, relies on imported iron and scrap metal: by shipping iron from the world's cheapest sources to industrial plants on the coast, the Japanese are able to produce steel which sells competitively.

Craft-based products

In many industrialized countries, machines have replaced craftsmen; not in Japan. Many everyday articles are made by hand, worked in wood, paper and bamboo by traditional methods. Even mass produced products often show the influence of these old crafts. Cheap pottery or printed cotton textiles are often beautifully designed.

▲ How a Japanese company looks after its employees. It is usual for a Japanese to spend his whole career in one company. He knows that promotion will come with time, rather than in recognition of ability. The company demands his loyalty and punctuality and in return offers the security of a retirement pension, assistance with housing and social and medical welfare.

▼ Rice is Japan's staple food and her chief agricultural product. Because Japan is mountainous, arable land is very limited. Farms are small and terraced fields are often carved out of the sides of mountains. Mechanization of farm implements and the practice of double cropping have helped to boost the harvest. The farming population has decreased dramatically since the War.

▲ A fishing fleet in port. Japan is one of the world's major fishing nations. Boats range from less than 10 tons for coastal fishing to a thousand tons for deep-sea trawling. There are many "fish-farms" where fish are artificially bred in shallow waters. Japan also has a thriving pearl industry.

◄ A television factory. Television sets are the chief consumer products of the electronics industry. Demand has increased rapidly since colour broadcasting began. Many electronic products are exported, especially radio receivers, colour television sets and desk computers.

▼ Assembly line in a car factory. In 1969 Japan's car industry was the second largest in the world after the United States. Many vehicles are exported, including "knock-down" cars, which are assembled abroad. The technical standard of car manufacture has risen considerably in recent years and Japanese cars have shown excellent performance in international racing competitions.

Traditional crafts

▲ A craft weaver at work. Japan has a fine tradition of weaving and dyeing silks and cottons.

▲ Hand-made paper has been produced in Japan for over a thousand years. Its uses range from art paper to fans and lacquered umbrellas.

▲ A craftsman making *tatami*, a household product still made by traditional methods. Mats have been used in Japanese houses for centuries.

Transport for a mobile nation

An efficient railway system

The Japanese enjoy a cheap and efficient system of public transport. The railway network carries more passengers than that of any other country. The biggest company is the national JNR which runs the fastest train service in the world between Tokyo and Okayama, on the New Tokaido Line. There are about 150 smaller private railways which run most of the local transport in and around the cities. Tokyo, Osaka, Nagoya, Kobe and Sapporo have underground railways and one is being constructed at Yokohama.

Some underground stations are linked to main line terminals to speed up the daily flow of commuters. The main line railways are so efficient that trains are punctual to the second. Loudspeakers on board keep passengers informed of the journey's progress, and there will be profuse apologies for a half minute delay!

Road travel

Comparatively few people travel by c But as roads improve, the railways gradually losing their monopoly of l distance transport. Within the towns bu and trams are the chief means of tra Taxis are plentiful and cheap, but passenger often has to act as navigator!

The Japanese are constantly experime ing with new and improved forms of tra port. The 210-kilometre-an-hour Bu train has been in operation for over a deca Monorail systems have been started different parts of the country. The first these was opened in Tokyo, when Olympic Games were held there in 1964 carries passengers 13 kilometres from airport into the city in 15 minutes. A n form of fast rail transport has just be developed which will cover the 500 ki metres (300 miles) between Tokyo a Osaka in one hour.

JAL is Japan's international airline. The present company was established in 1953 and international flights were started in 1954. Japan was six years behind the rest of the world in civil aviation, since she was forbidden to run an airline until the end of American occupation after the war. But she caught up rapidly and was the second country in the world to have an unbroken round-the-world service, linking Tokyo, New York and London. Jumbo jets were introduced to JAL's fleet in 1970. The 1975 fleet comprises 85 aircraft: 36 Boeing 747s, 47 DC-8s and 2 Japanese aircraft, YS-11. Two Concordes are on order for 1976.

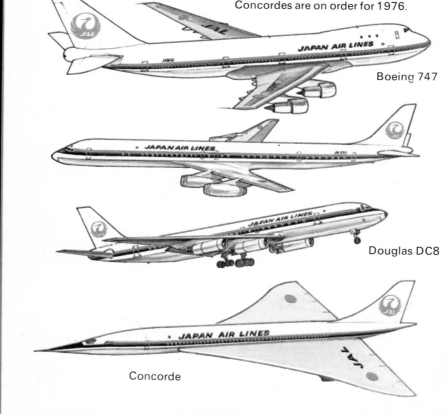

Boeing 747

Douglas DC8

Concorde

▼ An urban motorway. Road conditions have lagged behind the railways for years, but the position is changing now. The maj industrial cities of Tokyo, Nagoya and Kob are now linked and a complete national network is planned by 1985.

The Tokyo underground in the rush hour is notorious. The railway employs people to squash the passengers into the carriages (or pull them out!) so that the doors will shut. Passengers have been known to climb through the windows in the scramble.

▲ Passengers boarding the Bullet train, the world's fastest. Main line trains are designed so that when they pull up at the platform the doors are always in the same place. These points are marked and passengers queue up beside them.

▼ Japan has the world's second biggest merchant fleet. Shipping handles over a third of the nation's exports and nearly half its imports. There is a good network of coastal shipping, including several hovercraft and hydrofoil services.

Customs and festivals

New Year celebrations

Some people in Japan work six days a week. A few even work for seven! Shops are open on Sunday. But there are very many festivals, which are general holidays, in the year. New Year is to the Japanese what the Christmas holiday is to the West, and is the only time when everything closes down for a few days. At midnight on New Year's Eve people flock to the Shinto shrines to pray for health and prosperity. Many traditional foods are eaten; streets and homes are decorated with pine branches and ornaments of straw, and children fly kites.

Festival of the dead

Another important festival takes place in the summer. This is the *Bon* Festival, a day of worship for the dead. It is of Buddhist origin. The spirits of ancestors are believed to return to their old homes for a visit, and lighted paper lanterns are hung to guide them. Food is put out for them to eat. When the festival is over, bamboo and straw boats are floated down-river and out to sea, with candles to light the way back to the other world. Nowadays, at this festival, many people who have moved away from their home towns go back to visit them and their former neighbours.

The origins of many Japanese traditions lie in their ancient native religion, Shinto. Certain natural objects are worshipped, and thought to have magical powers. It is common to see huge trees decorated with straw ropes and streamers of white paper, and in the mountains tiny stone shrines with offerings of fresh flowers.

▼ Bathing is a leisurely and sociable activity for the Japanese. Working people look forward to a bath at the end of the day as a way of relaxing and shedding the tensions caused by city life.

▲ A wedding couple. The bride wears traditional costume and the bridegroom a formal Western suit. The wedding ceremony has no religious significance, but is often held at a Shinto shrine. Before the ceremony the bride is taken to the bridegroom's house by her parents and those responsible for arranging the marriage.

◄ The Japanese are great present givers. This is not usually a spontaneous gesture but part of a complicated social etiquette. Gifts must be returned and the reciprocating present must be carefully chosen so as not to offend the recipient either by being too meagre or so extravagant as to outdo the original gift.

▼ It is the custom to take off one's shoes on entering a house or a temple, or any building with polished wooden floors and *tatami*.

▲ A snake on the road is a lucky omen. Although in many legends the snake is a symbol of evil, it is also worshipped as a kindly deity. White snakes are especially sacred.

◄ A funeral. The funeral ceremony is a Buddhist rite which continues for several days after the cremation. A vigil beside the dead person is kept by relatives, friends and colleagues all night before the funeral.

▲ Women playing *Utagaruta,* a popular New Year card game: 100 poems are printed in separate halves on the cards and the game consists in matching the halves together as quickly as possible.

◄ A palanquin or portable shrine being carried at a festival. The covered shrine rests on long poles which lie along the shoulders of the carriers. It contains the spirit of the local deity.

▼ Huge carp streamers of paper or cloth are flown on May 5, the day of the Boys' Festival. The carp is a symbol of ambition and courage.

Buddhism and Shinto

▼ A Shinto priest or *Kannushi*. Shinto priests are appointed by the civil authorities. They may marry if they choose and their life style is no different from that of the rest of the people. Their duties are confined to reading the litanies and seeing to the repairs of the shrine. Their costume is an ancient court uniform.

The Way of the Gods

Shinto, Japan's ancient indigenous religion, is a form of nature worship. It was at first nameless but came to be called Shinto to distinguish it from Buddhism. The name is of Chinese origin, and means the "Way of the Gods". Shinto has many deities, known as *kami*.

According to Shinto belief the emperor is divine. The gods are rarely represented in human form. They are symbolized in the shrines by objects such as mirrors or swords. Shinto offers no philosophical system or moral code, but places great emphasis on fertility and ritual purity. It is not exclusive and many people who take part in its rites are also Buddhists.

Japanese Buddhism

Buddhism was introduced to Japan from China in 552 A.D. By the seventh century several sects were established; and by the ninth, Buddhism had greatly influenced Japanese culture. It adopted many native gods and beliefs from Shinto. Japanese Buddhism grew with the founding of numerous new sects. The two which are strongest today, *Jodo* (Pure Land) and *Shinshu* (True Sect) were founded in the twelfth century. They teach salvation through faith. Zen Buddhism, also from the twelfth century, took root among the *samurai*. It emphasizes self discipline. Zen means "meditation" but Zen philosophy is not opposed to action. It is anti-intellectual and relies on the personal transmission of truth from master to disciple.

Christianity was introduced to Japan in 1594 by the Jesuit missionary, St. Francis Xavier. Many Japanese became Christian in the following century. However, persecution and banishment by the military rulers caused Christianity to die out almost completely until the nineteenth century. A few determined converts secretly adhered to their religion, and their descendants still follow peculiar rites of their own. They are known as the *Kakure-Krishitan*, or hiding Christians.

▼ The *torii* (which means bird perch) marks the entrance to a Shinto shrine. *Torii* are usually made of wood and are often painted bright red. Some shrines have many *torii* forming a tunnel leading up to them. The biggest in Japan stands in the sea and is 16 metres high. Shinto shrines are often situated in places of great beauty.

▲ Worshippers at a Shinto shrine. Worship is simple and takes the form of hand-clapping, bowing and offerings of food, *sake* and money. The local shrine festival is a colourful occasion. Food stalls, markets and amusement booths are set up along the road leading to the shrine. People pay their respects to the local deity and *sake* is drunk freely.

The Religions of Japan

Source: Ministry of Foreign Affairs. Japan

Shinto	Buddhism	Christianity	Miscellaneous Religions
83 million	82 million	826,000	10 million adherents

▲ Most Japanese are Buddhists and many Japanese Buddhists are also members of the Shinto religion. The religions are not mutually exclusive. In fact many of their beliefs and practices have merged. Many new religions have sprung up in Japan in the last century and gained in popularity since the War. Tenrikyo is the oldest and largest of these. One of the newest is Sokka Gakkai, a political doctrine based on an old Buddhist sect.

▲ The 16 metre (53 feet) tall bronze Buddha, in the Todaiji temple at Nara. It was completed in 749 A.D. and is housed in the largest wooden building in the world.

► Ceremony in a Buddhist temple. Buddhism has a complex philosophy and moral code. It condemns killing and emphasizes the links between all things. "Everything is Buddha." Buddhist priests aspire to a state of Nirvana, the extinction of self and worldly desire.

Tokyo
the nerve-centre

Edo, the fishing village

Tokyo has not always been the capital of Japan. Originally Tokyo was a small fishing village called Edo. The capital was then several hundred miles to the west, first at Nara and then at Kyoto. However, at different periods in Japanese history the government moved near to Edo, though Kyoto remained the home of the court. In 1868 the capital was officially transferred to Edo. Edo was renamed Tokyo, which means "eastern capital".

Much of Tokyo was destroyed in the Kanto earthquake of 1923 and again during the Second World War. Today it is one of the largest, noisiest, most crowded cities in the world, and, at night especially, one of the gaudiest. By day concrete flyovers and office blocks seem to dwarf the wooden buildings, which themselves appear piled on top of one another. There seems to have been no attempt at planning. The city sprawls over much of the Kanto plain.

There is almost no greenery outside the few parks and the occasional tiny garden. By night Tokyo is alive with thousands of night clubs, cabarets and bars, and cinemas blazing with neon lights.

▲ Tokyo Tower has become the symbol of Japan's post-war material progress. It is a television pylon situated in Shiba park and is 332 metres high, 33 metres higher than the Eiffel Tower. The structure is designed to withstand earth tremors and typhoons.

▲ Tokyo devastated after the Kanto earthquake and fire of 1923. The earthquake occurred at eleven o'clock in the morning. People were thrown off their feet and tossed into the air. More than 110,000 people died.

◀ The Imperial Palace, in the heart of Tokyo, is surrounded by moats. It was formerly the castle of the Tokugawa military rulers. On New Year's Day, the public is admitted into the grounds to pay respects to, and be greeted by, the Emperor.

◄ Ueno market. Traditional life goes on, even in the centre of a modern metropolis. Some of Tokyo's residential neighbourhoods still retain the atmosphere of a small community.

▼ What to see in Tokyo. Since the city has been flattened twice in the last 50 years, by earthquake and war, there are few places of historic interest for sightseers. There are several "play areas" apart from Ginza, the most famous being Shinjuku.

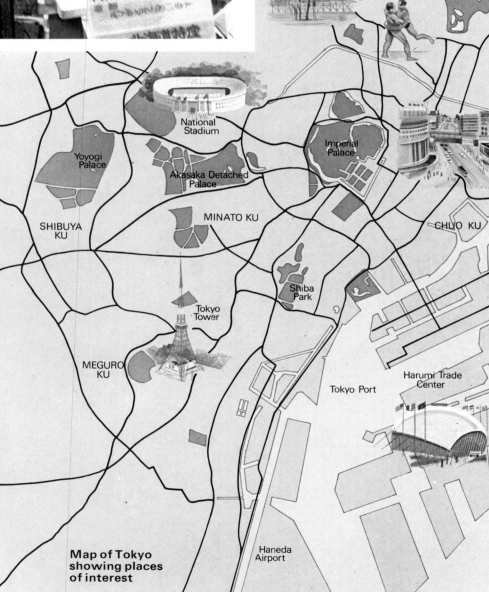

Map of Tokyo showing places of interest

The Ginza at night—Tokyo's most [fa]morous centre for shopping and night[...] Ginza means "silver mint," after the mint [coi]ned on that site in 1612. The present [Gin]za was the first street in Japan with brick [buil]dings and pavements.

The feudal era

The great shogun

Tokugawa Ieyasu was a strong military ruler, or *shogun*, who gave his name to a remarkable period of Japanese history. He was responsible, after two other men, Nobunaga and Hideyoshi, for bringing peace and unity to Japan after over a century of civil war. He defeated his rivals and became *shogun* in 1603. He abdicated in favour of his son, Hidetada, but kept the real power, and formed a system of administration that lasted two and a half centuries.

The *Shogunate* (or government) of the Tokugawa family devised a number of ways to control the country. The most powerful men in society were the *daimyo*, or territorial lords. They had their own private armies and had caused ruin by warring among themselves. The government kept troublesome lords in check by placing friendly *daimyo* near them.

Controlling the powerful lords

All lords had to pay regular homage to the *shogun* and attend the *shogun*'s headquarters for several months, or a year, at a time. Moreover their wives and families had to stay permanently in Edo. This system impoverished the *daimyo*, who not only had to keep two households but had to pay for the regular journey of an entire retinue. They were often called on to carry out expensive public works. To make quite sure they didn't misbehave, spies watched them both at Edo and at their homes.

One remarkable feature of Tokugawa rule was the closing of Japan to the outside world. Foreign missionaries were expelled, and Christianity suppressed. By 1638, citizens were forbidden to leave the country on pain of death. The only foreigners allowed on Japanese soil were Chinese and Dutch traders, and they had to stay at the port of Nagasaki in the south.

It was probably this isolation from foreign influence which enabled the rigid, but peaceful and stable, society to survive unchanged for so long.

▲ From 1490 to 1590 the *daimyo* fought to dominate the land. Oda Nobunaga was first to gain partial success. Unification was completed by his general, Hideyoshi. Tokugawa Ieyasu gained power after Hideyoshi's death.

◀ Osaka castle. Castles were built as the seats of *daimyo*, and towns grew up around them. Osaka castle was the stronghold of Ieyasu's last rival, Hideyoshi's son. It was taken by storm in 1616 after a long and bitter siege. The surviving occupants committed suicide.

▼ Tokugawa Ieyasu started his military career in Nobunaga's army. He was small but powerful and combined unshakeable patience with political foresight.

Tokugawa Ieyasu

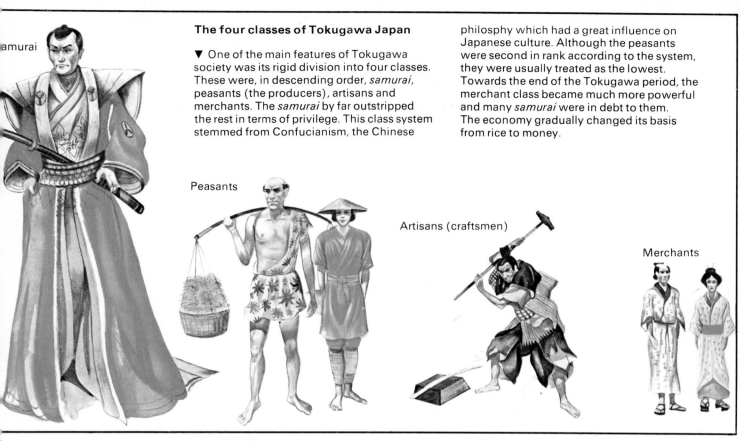

The four classes of Tokugawa Japan

▼ One of the main features of Tokugawa society was its rigid division into four classes. These were, in descending order, *samurai*, peasants (the producers), artisans and merchants. The *samurai* by far outstripped the rest in terms of privilege. This class system stemmed from Confucianism, the Chinese philosphy which had a great influence on Japanese culture. Although the peasants were second in rank according to the system, they were usually treated as the lowest. Towards the end of the Tokugawa period, the merchant class became much more powerful and many *samurai* were in debt to them. The economy gradually changed its basis from rice to money.

samurai

Peasants

Artisans (craftsmen)

Merchants

A *daimyo* procession making its way to ▷ to pay homage to the *shogun*. The main tes to Edo were thronged with these ular processions. The Tokaido road, from oto and the west, was made famous by the nts of Hiroshige illustrating the 53 resting ces along the way.

▶ Ieyasu's impressive mausoleum in the mountains at Nikko. Because he brought peace and security to Japan, he has been revered as a national hero. His posthumous title is *Tosho Gongen*, ''Buddha Incarnate as Sun God of the East.'' Ieyasu's achievement draws thousands of visitors to his shrine.

The Meiji restoration

▲ The arrival of Matthew Perry's ships in 1853. Perry brought a request from the American President that Japan reopen her ports to foreign trade. A year later the Japanese rulers were forced into agreement.

▼ Meiji rulers mix with members of the old order. The Meiji leaders (in Western dress) were mainly young ex-*samurai*. Their policies differed from those of the Tokugawa regime, but their form of government—group rule—remained the same.

Meiji Rule

In 1866 the rule of the Tokugawa family was overthrown by a group of *samurai* leaders from Satsuma and Choshu. Social and economic changes had been taking place below the surface in Tokugawa Japan, and by the nineteenth century the old system was no longer adequate. The government had not been able to ward off Perry's ships, nor to keep out the influence of America and Europe.

The *samurai* revolution and the period following is known as the Meiji Restoration, called after the reigning emperor Meiji. This title means "Enlightened Rule". The new policy was to restore authority, if not political power, to the emperor, and to combat the threat of the West by taking over Western skills and weapons. The slogan was "A prosperous nation, strongly armed".

Modernizing Japan

A period of modernization began in which education, industry, communications and the armed forces were built up on the Western model. The old *daimyo* domains were replaced with prefectures (*ken*) under the control of the new capital, Tokyo. The *samurai* class lost its privileges, and military conscription was introduced. Feudal class distinctions were abolished. The political

and legal systems were reformed to gain t[he] approval and recognition of Western powe[rs.] Japan's rigid administration, with lit[tle] experience of dealing with the outsi[de] world, had been forced to sign tradi[ng] treaties with Western nations, which alwa[ys] gave Japan the worse bargain. A new co[n]stitution was proclaimed in 1889. This h[ad] as its basis the absolute sovereignty of t[he] emperor, who was stated to be "sacred a[nd] inviolable".

Growth of the Japanese Empire

By the end of the nineteenth century, Jap[an] had become strong enough to challenge a[nd] defeat China and Russia in war. In 190[?,] before the Russian war, she made an allian[ce] with Britain. She was fast becoming a wo[rld] power with a growing colonial empire.

Meanwhile, at home, living conditio[ns] did not improve as industry progresse[d,] because profits were ploughed back in[to] machinery or weapons. Housing and fo[od] were poor, and wages low. Industry w[as] dominated by a few giant corporations, [or] *zaibatsu*, closely supported by the gover[n]ment. The growth of industry brought wi[th] it a new urban class. The educated whi[te] collar worker was called a "salary-man", [a] term used to this day.

The emperor Meiji died in 1912.

▲ The Meiji leaders brought about a revolution in daily life. As part of their rapid modernization programme, they opened Japan's first railway line in 1872. It ran between Tokyo and Yokohama. In a few ye[ars] several lines were operating at a profit.

44

The Emperor Meiji listens while his Charter Oath of Five Articles is read. This document was issued in 1868 and was the first step towards democracy, promising government by consent.

The interior of a spinning factory. The cotton spinning industry was the first to apply mass production techniques. Other light industries soon followed. The Meiji rulers saw industrialization as a source of funds to build up military power.

▲ The new army was modelled on those of the West. Conscription was introduced in 1872. By 1876 *samurai* were no longer allowed to wear swords. A strong navy was built up on the lines of the British navy and many officers were British trained.

The spread of Japanese military influence

▲ Japanese troops advancing in the Russo-Japanese war of 1904–5. Russia was defeated on sea and land.

Growth of the Empire

Hokkaido

Korea annexed 1910

Port Arthur

Tokyo

Japan

Yellow Sea

Korea Strait

Formosa annexed 1895

▲ The Japanese empire at the end of the Meiji period. Japan was to make further gains in the First World War.

▲ The Japanese army besieging Peking in the Boxer Rising of 1900. Japanese troops helped to rescue the legations in Peking.

Hirohito war and peace

The army takes control

The 1920s, when Emperor Hirohito came to the throne, were years of depression and insecurity in Japan, as they were everywhere in the world. In 1923 most of Tokyo was destroyed by earthquake and fire. At the end of the decade incidents in Manchuria showed that the army had become dangerously powerful and was pushing for further military expansion. In February 1936 several chief government members were assassinated by a group of extremist officers, and in 1941 General Tojo became Prime Minister. The government was now in the hands of the army, and laws were passed to repress opposition to its aggressive colonialist policies.

When France surrendered to Hitler, Japan took over French colonies in Asia, and formed a full alliance with Germany and Italy. Starting with the surprise attack on Pearl Harbour in 1941, Japan had a series of dramatic victories in Malaya, Hong Kong, Singapore, Burma and the Pacific islands. Her fortune changed after 1942, when the Americans and Allied forces began to win back these territories and to close in on Japan itself. Air raids on Japanese cities began. The Japanese surrendered only after two cities had been destroyed by atomic bombs. Their desperate attempts at resistance included the dive bombing of American ships at Okinawa by suicide pilots. The emperor broadcast the decision to surrender on August 14, 1945.

Peace and reconstruction

American occupation after the war was peaceful and constructive. The new constitution of 1947 renounced war, and the emperor's authority was reduced. He became a "symbol of the state and of the unity of the people".

The transition from occupation to independence went hand in hand with economic recovery and progress. The Japanese have always been prepared to work hard, and have unusual ability to learn technical skills. By the end of the fifties Japan was the third largest economic power in the world, after the United States and Russia.

▼ The present emperor, Hirohito, as a young man. He was born in 1901. After completing his education, he spent six months travelling in Europe. He became Prince Regent in 1921 and succeeded to the throne in 1926 on the death of his father, the emperor Taisho. The present "year period" which began with his rule is named *Showa*, "Radiant Peace". By the time Hirohito came to the throne, Japan had universal male suffrage and a party political system.

▲ An Italian poster celebrating Japan's victories in the Pacific. The thirties had been decade of military aggression abroad and murderous violence at home.

▼ The first atomic bomb was dropped on Hiroshima on August 6, 1945. The city was obliterated. Scientists predicted that nothing would grow there for 70 years. Within three years trees were budding again. Today Hiroshima is a thriving city.

▼ A modern Japanese bank. Before the end of the fifties Japan boasted the third largest economy in the world after the United States and Russia.

▲ In March 1970 EXPO '70 was opened in Osaka. This was the first time a world exhibition had been held in Asia. After years of hard work and over-sensitive reaction on the subjects of war and nationalism, Japan appeared to the rest of the world as a country full of confidence in its own image.

▼ Emperor Hirohito with his family today. He has six children: two sons and four daughters. He is a keen student of marine biology and has published several books on the subject. In 1946 Emperor Hirohito made a personal broadcast to the people renouncing his divine status.

Heroes of honour

The virtue of loyalty

Japan has a wealth of legend, and has a dynamic, violent history. These have inspired much of her art and literature. Yet she has produced few outstanding heroes. This may be because the Japanese give less importance to individuality than do Western societies. The tendency is to conform to the character of one's group rather than develop one's individual personality. The influence of Buddhism has probably strengthened this impersonality.

One of the most famous heroic legends concerns not one man but forty-seven! The incident of the Forty-seven Ronin shook Tokugawa Japan and became a favourite theme of playwrights. Asano Naganori, a *daimyo*, drew his sword under severe provocation in Edo castle and wounded an official of the *shogun*. Since merely to draw one's sword within the castle grounds meant the death penalty, Asano was compelled to commit suicide. His forty-seven *samurai* (*ronin* means masterless *samurai*) vowed vengeance on the official who had caused their lord's death. To avoid suspicion, they scattered and lay low, pretending to sink into lives of debauchery. Suddenly they stormed the official's home during a banquet, cut off his head and placed it on Asano's tomb. They surrendered to the officers of justice and in their turn were made to commit suicide. They became heroes since they died honourably, their loyalty representing the highest feudal virtue. Their tombs are in the temple of Sen-gakuji in Tokyo.

▲ Kobo Daishi (774-835 A.D.) is Japan's most famous and beloved Buddhist saint. He introduced an important sect of Buddhism, Shingon, to Japan from China. He founded the monastery on Mount Koya which became the headquarters of the sect. Today Kobo Daishi's name is a household word. He is remembered as a scholar, poet, artist, explorer and calligrapher. Several inventions are attributed to him, including the Japanese phonetic alphabet. He was responsible for many miracles and a type of bamboo forest is said to have sprung from his walking cane.

Prince Genji

▶ Prince Genji is the hero of a romantic novel written in the eleventh century A.D. by a court lady named Murasaki Shikibu. It is considered by many to be the greatest work of literature in Japanese history. The mood of the book is one of sweet melancholy and nostalgia. The ideal hero embodied in Genji was sensitive, refined, gallant and accomplished in the arts, especially poetry. He had none of the ascetic military virtues found later in the *samurai* code. A typical love affair would be started by a signal as subtle as the glimpse of a sleeve from a carriage window or the sound of a lute playing.

▲ A dramatic moment in the Kabuki play about the 47 Ronin. Asano prepares to commit *hara-kiri* in the presence of his forty-seven retainers.

▼ There is a legend which tells of an old man who performed a miracle with watermelons. One summer's day a caravan was taking a load of melons to market. The drivers stopped to quench their thirst with a melon. Just then the old man appeared and humbly asked them for a piece. They refused, so the old man sowed the melon seeds and instantly new plants grew up. Everyone ate their fill. When the drivers set off again, they discovered that every one of their melons had vanished.

▲ Saigo Takamori (1827-1877) was a rebel in the Meiji government. He championed the cause of the *samurai* and peasant classes whose way of life was threatened by the new Meiji policies. In 1877 he led an armed rebellion in Satsuma, his native province. The rebellion was suppressed after months of fighting, with many thousands killed. Saigo was wounded in battle and beheaded on request by a friend. "The great Saigo" was a big man with a strong character. He represents the last stand of the old feudal order in Japan and his statue stands in Ueno Park in Tokyo. He was a fierce nationalist, but he has become a hero, probably because the feudal age is viewed with nostalgia.

▲ Many adult comics are published in Japan, with heroes both traditional and Western.

The Japanese character

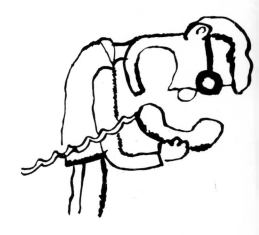

The family and the nation

The Japanese has a strong sense of belonging to a group whose interests override his own. Japanese society is made up of many groups, from the family to the most important group of all, the nation. Moral standards are based on conventions, rather than on principles; a person may behave quite differently at home and outside.

The group is rather like a pyramid, in which everyone feels responsible for those above and below them. There are two words, seldom spoken, but kept in mind none the less, which explain this pyramid. The first, *giri*, means the duty of the individual to others, or the "right thing to do". For example, a whole community would feel obliged to help an orphan or a widow. Failure to do this would cause grave offence.

The other idea, *on*, expresses obligation to superiors. People are expected to acknowledge their debt to parents, teachers, employers, and the gods. It expresses humility and dependence. There is a saying in Japanese: "Everyone is a debtor to the world". Old people are always honoured and cared for.

This need to belong explains some of the characteristics of the Japanese. They hate to be laughed at, or singled out in any way. Even in business, ties of loyalty are very important. The notion of business being controlled by laws and contracts is strange to the Japanese. They are also very emotional, and their hearts often rule their heads. Japanese people are often sentimental, and can enjoy themselves with great abandon. Calmness and harmony are high ideals; and much self discipline is needed to achieve the passionless facade that Orientals seem to show outsiders.

▲ A Japanese employee bows mechanically to his boss, even on the telephone. The Japanese are always conscious of rank. Even among apparent equals there are subtle differences, such as age or seniority at work. But there is no permanent class distinction, since people can move up and down the hierarchy. They are all parts of the same pyramid. Even the word for gods, *kami*, simply means superior. The language has different forms of addressing people according to their position on the social scale.

▶ The tea ceremony (*chanoyu*) developed under the influence of Zen Buddhism. It shows how Japanese people find or create beauty in plainness and simplicity. The ceremony is performed according to rules which have not changed since the sixteenth century. The setting and the utensils must be simple but beautiful and the serving and drinking of the tea should be done with pleasing economy of movement. All the details of the ceremony are consciously appreciated by those taking part.

The Japanese are very nationalistic. They ometimes seem obsessed by the image of apan as she appears to the world.

''Them and us'' mentality. A man who ghts a stranger for a seat will give it up for omeone he knows, especially a superior.

▲ The Japanese are fond of working hard. The average employee is such an integral part of his company that he feels that he is working for himself and his fellow workers rather than for a separate boss.

▶ The most popular form of suicide for frustrated young couples is to throw themselves into volcanoes. The Japanese commit suicide for reasons puzzling to Westerners. They like to feel themselves swept along by a higher force, a sentiment which transcends fear of death.

The Japanese love festivals. Here, a float earing a portable shrine is drawn through e streets of Kyoto at the annual Gion festival.

Working women gossiping by the road- de. They may be gardeners or roadsweepers. omen in Japan often do light manual out- oor work. Their clothes, like most Japanese orking clothes, derive from the traditional ess worn by farmers and peasants.

Facing the future

The energetic Japanese

The Japanese have a great capacity for change and renewal. They live in a land where earthquakes and typhoons can destroy the work of centuries in as many minutes. So they have had to learn to be prepared to begin again.

In this century Japan has already changed amazingly. After defeat in the last war the people poured the energy which had gone into military conquest into peaceful growth.

The new prosperity and "Americanization" brought many social changes. The position of women has become freer than it was. They have cheap electrical gadgets to save time and labour in housework. Women are no longer restricted by traditional clothes, which made their movements, and their gestures, affectedly over-dainty. Now, husbands treat their wives less like property, and more like life-partners. Families are smaller, and working hours are gradually becoming shorter.

People are growing taller and living longer now that the national diet has changed to include more protein, and fats from dairy products. The Japanese are slowly becoming more cosmopolitan, but insularity lingers, and foreigners are still stared at.

New problems

Industrial growth, which has brought with it so many improvements, is now confronting Japan with a new crisis. The world is running short of natural resources, and pollution is spreading its poison. Japan relies on selling products made from imported raw materials, so it is worse affected by shortages than many other advanced nations. Pollution in Japan has caused terrible new diseases for which there is no known cure.

The Japanese are very aware of their problems. Some people believe the answer lies in the return to older values. No one knows what the solution will be, but if any people can find one, it will be the Japanese, with their enormous energy, diligence, and adaptability.

▲ A sign of Japan's new industrial prosperity is the increasing number of people who are travelling abroad, both on business and on holiday.

▼ Striking workers on the march. Japanese businessmen are said to have visited Western countries to study the methods of the strike! Traditionally, strikes are rare in Japan, apart from the annual "spring struggle". This is an orderly token gesture by employees which accompanies the yearly wage review. Workers belong to company (rather than industry-wide) unions.

▼ Dock worker in Yokohama wearing a smog mask. Pollution has become a serious problem. Most city centres have an electronic pollution indicator which displays the level of noise and carbon monoxide. Traffic police in Tokyo are equipped with oxygen masks. Coastal fishing is suffering from the effects of water pollution caused by effluent from factories and the cities.

► World inflation and the rising cost of raw materials and fuel are threatening the economy. America has already begun to discriminate against Japanese goods. Japan has a population of over 100 million and few natural resources of her own.

Fuel and trade problems

How Japanese living standards have risen

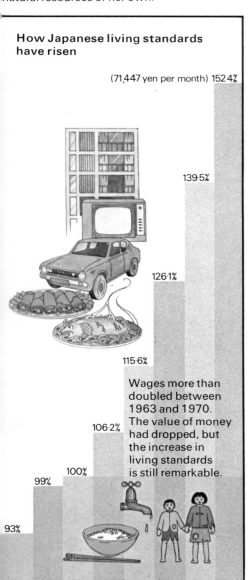

(71,447 yen per month) 152·4%

139·5%

126·1%

115·6%

Wages more than doubled between 1963 and 1970. The value of money had dropped, but the increase in living standards is still remarkable.

106·2%

100%

99%

93%

| 1963 | 1964 | 1965 | 1966 | 1967 | 1968 | 1969 | 1970 |

▲ For a long time, while industry expanded, wages stood still. Mass unemployment after the War kept pay low. By 1960 labour was getting scarce and since then wages have been rising by more than 10 per cent a year. Today for the first time they are comparable to those of Western Europe. Although still careful savers, the Japanese have departed somewhat from their traditional austerity and are spending more money on consumer goods and entertainment.

► Since 1959 Japan has been the world's leading shipbuilder. The biggest tankers ever built have come from her shipyards.

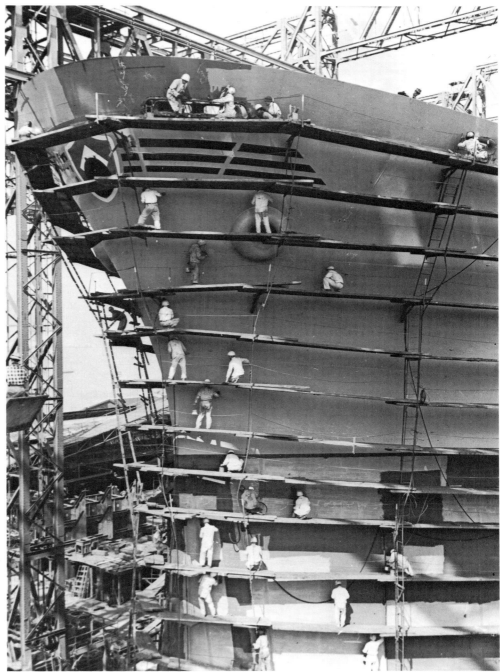

Reference
Human and physical geography

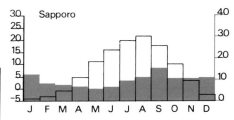

The climate of Japan

Sapporo

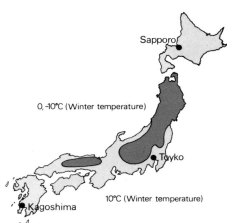

0, -10°C (Winter temperature)

10°C (Winter temperature)

Sapporo

Tokyo

Kagoshima

CLIMATE

Japan is in the temperate zone at the north-eastern end of the monsoon area covering Korea, China, Southeast Asia and India. The climate varies throughout Japan, due to the continental air current from the north west and the oceanic air current from the southeast. Temperature and humidity are high in summer, low in winter. June is the rainy season. September brings typhoons.

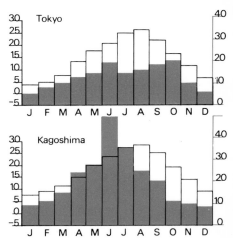

Tokyo

Kagoshima

FACTS AND FIGURES
THE LAND AND PEOPLE

Position: Japan is made up of four main islands—Hokkaido, Honshu, Shikoku and Kyushu—and more than 3,000 islets. The archipelago stretches in an arc along the north eastern Pacific coast of the Asian continent. The northern island of Hokkaido is less than 45 kilometres from Sakhalin and the southern island of Kyushu is 200 kilometres from Korea.

Area: Japan's total area is 377,389 square kilometres (145,670 square miles). Area of main islands: Honshu 230,822 square km, Hokkaido 83,511, Kyushu 42,030, Shikoku 18,782.

Topography: Japan has a long, rocky coastline and many mountains, valleys, rivers and lakes. Highest mountain is Fuji, 3,776 metres (12,389 ft). There are 196 volcanoes, of which 30 are active. These provide mineral hot springs which feed many spa resorts, but also cause frequent earth tremors and occasional earthquakes.

Administration: Japan is divided into 47 prefectures, including Tokyo Metropolitan District.

Population: 107,332,000 in 1972. Honshu: 85,191,000 and Tokyo: 10,348,975 at the last census.

Flag: Solid red circle on white background. Called *Hi-no Maru*, which means "Circle of the sun". Symbolic of Japan, Nippon meaning "Source of the sun".

Anthem: Kimigayo (The reign of our Emperor), since 1888. Words from an ancient poem.

Imperial family: Emperor Hirohito is 124th in imperial line. In the Constitution he is "the symbol of the state and of the unity of the people, deriving his position from the will of the people with whom resides sovereign power".

Armed forces: No army, since the Constitution renounces war. But a Self-defence force and a collective security system with the U.S.

International organizations: Member of the U.N. since 1956. Since 1953 member of U.N. Economic Commission for Asia and the Far East (ECAFE). Member of Asian and Pacific Council (ASPAC), GATT and OECD.

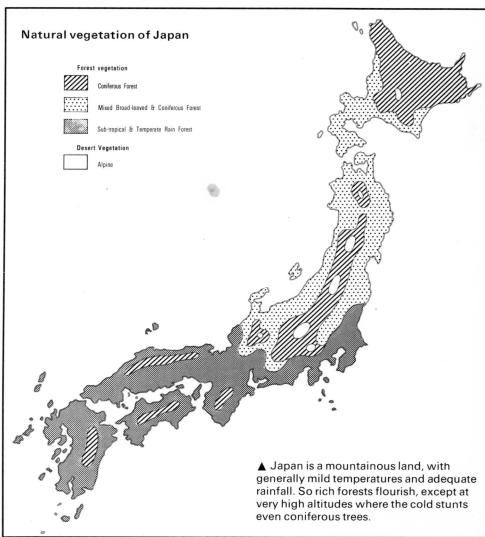

Natural vegetation of Japan

Forest vegetation

- Coniferous Forest
- Mixed Broad-leaved & Coniferous Forest
- Sub-tropical & Temperate Rain Forest

Desert Vegetation

- Alpine

▲ Japan is a mountainous land, with generally mild temperatures and adequate rainfall. So rich forests flourish, except at very high altitudes where the cold stunts even coniferous trees.

Inhabitants	
per mile²	per km²
under 32	under 12
32-64	12-25
64-128	25-50
128-256	50-100
256-512	100-200
over 512	over 200

Government

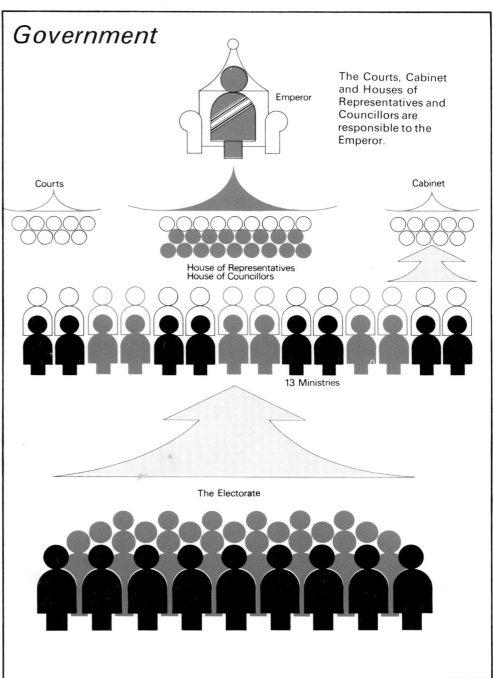

Emperor

The Courts, Cabinet and Houses of Representatives and Councillors are responsible to the Emperor.

Courts

Cabinet

House of Representatives
House of Councillors

13 Ministries

The Electorate

POPULATION

he census has been taken regularly since 721. From a stable 30 million in the okugawa period, the population rose apidly with industrialization, almost tripling etween 1872 and 1970. Japan today has he sixth largest population in the world after ndonesia, the United States, the U.S.S.R., ndia and China. Japan is densely populated 284 persons per square kilometre, or 737 er square mile) and population is unevenly istributed. About 70 per cent live in cities nd of these 58 per cent are in the "Big our" areas around Tokyo, Osaka, Nagoya nd Kitakyushu. Medium sized cities such as apporo, Sendai and Hiroshima, are rowing rapidly. The birth rate, which rose fter the War, has now dropped to one of the owest in the world. The death rate has also ropped, with life expectancy 20 years onger than in 1935. Population structure as changed to include an ever-increasing roportion of old people.

THE MAJOR TOWNS

Japan has several large towns, some very congested, because the mountains prevent expansion.

The most important are given below, with their population size in 1965.

Tokyo	10,348,975
Osaka	3,156,201
Nagoya	1,935,430
Yokohama	1,788,796
Kyoto	1,364,977
Kobe	1,216,579
Kitakyushu	1,042,389

GOVERNMENT

Under the Constitution of 1947, Japan renounced war and the divine status of the emperor. Sovereignty rests with the people. Fundamental human rights are guaranteed as eternal and inviolable. The parliamentary system is based on the three powers of legislature, executive and judiciary.

The Legislature: The Diet is the sole law-making body. It consists of the House of Representatives with 491 seats and the House of Councillors with 252 seats. Members are elected for 4 and 6 years respectively by all people over 20 years old.

The Executive: The chief executive is the Prime Minister who is elected by the Diet from its members and who appoints the 19 Cabinet Ministers. A vote of no confidence in the Diet may force the Cabinet to resign. But the Prime Minister may instead dissolve the House of Representatives and call a general election.

The Judiciary: The Judiciary is independent of the Diet and the Cabinet. The Supreme Court has a Chief Justice and 14 other justices. Their appointment is reviewed by the people in periodic referenda.

Local government: The 47 prefectures, as well as cities, towns and villages, have local assemblies whose members are elected by voters in the community.

Political parties: Besides the ruling Liberal-Democratic Party (conservative), there are three major opposition parties: the Socialist Party, the Democratic-Socialist Party and the Communist Party.

Reference
History

Main Events in Japanese History

50,000 B.C. Paleolithic culture.
8,000 B.C. Jomon culture.
300 B.C. Yayoi culture.
57 A.D. Envoy to the Han court (China) from Japanese kingdom of Nu.
300 Tomb culture.
400— Emergence of Yamato Imperial clan.
552 Introduction of Buddhism to Japan.
562 Rising Korean kingdom of Silla destroys Japanese power in Korea.
592— Reign of Suiko and Regent
628 Shotoku Taishi.
594 Buddhism proclaimed state religion.
607 First Japanese embassy to China.
645 Taika Reform. Introduction of Chinese system of administration and land redistribution.
702 Promulgation of Taiho Code.

NARA PERIOD
710 Capital established at Nara.

HEIAN PERIOD
794 Capital moved to Kyoto (Heian-kyo).
812 Final subjugation of Ainu in north.
838 Last official mission to Tang China.
858 Beginning of Fujiwara family regency.
897— "Golden" reign of Emperor Daigo.
930 Suspension of Fujiwara regency.
939— Military disturbances in provinces.
1088 Emergence of warrior *samurai*.
1068 Emperor Go-Sanjo and attempt to curb Fujiwara power.
1159 Taira Kiyomori, provincial military aristocrat, takes control of Kyoto and government.

KAMAKURA PERIOD
1185 Defeat of Taira clan. Minamoto Yoritomo supreme in Japan.
1192 Yoritomo becomes *shogun* (military ruler).
1199 Yoritomo dies. Start of Hojo Regency.
1221 Unsuccessful attempt by cloistered Emperor Go-Toba to destroy Hojo.
1274— Unsuccessful Mongol invasions.
1281 Japan aided by "Divine Winds" (*Kamikaze*) typhoons.
1333 End of Hojo Regency. Emperor Go-Daigo institutes direct imperial rule.

ASHIKAGA or MUROMACHI PERIOD
1338 Ashikaga Takauji becomes *shogun*.
1467 Onin civil war. First of more than a century of civil wars. Growth of new *daimyo* (warlord) class and autonomous domains. Peasant uprisings. Breakdown of law and order.
1543 First Europeans (Portuguese) visit Japan. Missionaries and traders.
1549 St. Francis Xavier reaches Japan.

PERIOD OF UNIFICATION
1568 Nobunaga controls capital.
1571 Power of large Buddhist monasteries cut down.
1582 Nobunaga assassinated. Toyotomi takes over.
1587 First persecution of Christians.
1587 Whole country under Hideyoshi's control. Establishment of fixed social order (separation of warriors and farmers).
1592 First of Hideyoshi's Korean expeditions.
1597 Second Korean expedition, and failure.
1598 Hideyoshi dies.

TOKUGAWA PERIOD
1600 Victory of Tokugawa Ieyasu at Sekigahara.
c.1600 Arrival of first Dutch and British.
1603 Establishment of Tokugawa military rule. Strict social ordering. Control of *daimyo* by enforced periodic attendance on *shogun*.
1615 Destruction of Toyotomi family at Osaka castle.
1617 Further Christian persecutions.
1624 Spaniards expelled.
1637 Shimabara revolt. Christians and rebels wiped out.
1639 Last of the Seclusion edicts. Foreigners limited to Dutch and Chinese at Nagasaki. No Japanese to leave (or return) on pain of death.
1700— Discontent within Tokugawa system. Social disorder. Growing economic power of merchant class, poverty of *samurai* and farmers.
1703 Incident of 47 Ronin.
1715 Yoshimune becomes shogun. Attempts to reform system.
1732 Great famine.
1783— 86 Serious famines and epidemics.
1789 Reforms of Matsudaira Sadanobu.
18C8 British warship at Nagasaki. Early western attempts to pierce Japan's isolation.
1830 Reforms of Mizuno Tadakuni. Similar to earlier unsuccessful ones. Tokugawa system collapsing.
1837 U.S. Mercy ship at Uraga.
1853 Arrival of Perry and the "Black ships".
1854 Treaty of Friendship with U.S.
1863 British fleet attacks Kagoshima.
1864 Combined British, Dutch and French fleet destroy Choshu forts.
1867 Abolition of shogunate. Causes: foreign military threat, powerful *daimyo* of western Japan, peasant unrest, desire to restore "Imperial rule", and breakdown of Tokugawa social and economic system.

MEIJI PERIOD
1867 Emperor Meiji ascends the throne.
1868 Transfer of imperial capital to Edo, renamed Tokyo.
1869 Abolition of feudal domains and start of Japan's modernization.
1871 Feudal four-class system abolished. Conscript army formed.
1874 First popular Assembly.
1876 Satsuma rebellion of *samurai*.
1889 Prince Ito's Constitution; limited suffrage.
1894—5 Sino-Japanese war: Japanese victory.
1902 Anglo-Japanese Alliance.
1904—5 Russo-Japanese war: Japan wins with ease.
1910 Annexation of Korea.

TAISHO PERIOD
1912 Death of Meiji. Accession of Taisho.
1914 Japan enters 1st World War with Britain, France and Russia.
1918 Riots over price of rice.
1919 Japan a signatory of Versailles Treaty.
1920 Japan joins League of Nations.
1921 Hirohito becomes regent.
1923 Kanto earthquake.
1925 Universal adult male suffrage.

SHOWA PERIOD
1926 Death of Taisho. Accession of Hirohito.
1931 Japanese take control of Manchuria.
1933 League of Nations oppose Japanese action in Manchuria. Japan withdraws from League.
1936 Government officials murdered by military. New cabinet dominated by army.
1937 Invasion of China. Sack of Nanking.
1940 Alliance with Germany and Italy.
1941 Pearl Harbour. Japan destroys U.S. fleet, leading to war with U.S., Britain, Netherlands.
1945 Japan defeated. American occupation.
1947 New Constitution. Women get the vote.
1951 Peace Treaty of San Francisco.
1952 End of American occupation.
1956 Diplomatic relations with U.S.S.R. restored. Japan joins United Nations.
1964 Olympic Games held in Tokyo.
1968 Ogasawara Island restored to Japan.
1970 Expo 70 in Osaka.
1971 United States imposes import surcharge on Japanese goods.
1972 Okinawa restored to Japan. Renewed relations with China. Winter Olympic Games in Sapporo.
1974 Prime Minister Tanaka forced to resign.

The Arts

ARCHAIC PERIOD (before 555 A.D.)
Pottery: from 8000 B.C. Jomon hand-built pottery with "rope pattern" surface decoration. From c. 390 B.C., Yayoi wheel-thrown pottery. From c. 300 A.D., Tomb culture pottery figurines called Haniwa.
Architecture: Tomb culture Shinto architecture, showing "South Seas" influence: Izumo and Ise shrines.

ASUKA PERIOD (552–645)
Architecture: First surviving Buddhist temple, Horyuji, near Nara.
Sculpture: Wooden and bronze sculpture Tori school.
Painting: Religious, on doors and panels of Tamamushi-zushi, miniature shrine in Horyuji.

NARA PERIOD (645–794)
Architecture: Building of monasteries. Toshodaiji, pagoda of Yakushiji. Shosoin repository of decorative arts.
Sculpture: Giant Buddhas in bronze, clay and hollow dry lacquer: bronze 16 metre high seated Buddha in the Todaiji, Nara. Thousand armed Kannon of Toshodaiji.
Painting: Frescoes of Buddhist Paradise in Horyuji. "Sutras of Past and Present Karma", oldest preserved scrolls.
Literature: Man'yoshu, anthology of 4,500 Japanese poems; appearance of *waka* form (alternating 5 and 7 syllable lines). Kaifuso, anthology of Chinese style poems. 712 A.D., *Kojiki* (Record of Ancient Matters) in Japanese. 720 A.D. *Nihon-shoki* (Chronicles of Japan) in Chinese.

HEIAN PERIOD (974–1185)
Architecture: Shinden-zukuri, building-and-garden complex. Phoenix Hall, Ho-odo, Uji, near Kyoto. Five storied pagoda, Daigoji, near Kyoto. Kasuga shrine, Nara. 816 A.D. monastery built on Koya-san by Kukai (Kobo Daishi).
Sculpture: Shaka and Kannon statues, Muroji, near Nara. Amida by Jocho in Phoenix Hall. Eleven headed Kannon in Rokkeji.
Painting: Beginning of landscape painting. Mandalas, symbolic representations of the universe. Calligraphy. Beginning of secular art in Yamato-e, narrative scrolls in native style of painting: Tale of Genji scroll.
Literature: 905 A.D., Kokinshu, anthology of aristocratic poetry. Tale of Genji by Murasaki Shikibu (c.978–c.1031), world's first great novel; aesthetic principle of *aware*. *Makura no soshi* (Pillow Book) by Sei Shonagon (c.966–c.1013), commentary on court life; aesthetic principle of *okashi*.

KAMAKURA PERIOD (1185–1333)
Architecture: New style of Zen architecture: Nanzenji, Daitokuji, Kenninji, in Kyoto. Kenchoji and Engakuji in Kamakura.
Sculpture: Golden age of sculpture, beginning with Kokei: bronze 13 metre high Amida Buddha at Kamakura. Wooden religious images and portrait statues of Unkei and his school.
Painting: E-makimono (illustrated scrolls) depicting warfare (Heiji Monogatari), and lives of Buddhist priests. Portrait of Yoritomo. The Tosa school.
Literature: Shinkokinshu, poetry anthology including outstanding *waka* poetry by priest Saigyo (1118–1190). New genre of war tales, Heike Monogatari. *Hojoki* (Account of my Hut) by Kamo no Chomei. *Tsurezuregusa* (Essays in Idleness) by Yoshida Kenko (1283–1350). Fujiwara Teika (1162–1242), poet and compiler of Shinkokinshu.

MUROMACHI PERIOD (1333–1568)
Architecture: Kinkakuji (Golden Pavilion) built 1397 and Ginkakuji (Silver Pavilion), Kyoto.
Painting: Zen inspired black and white ink painting: Sesshu (1420–1506), Josetsu, Shobun, Sesson. The Kano family—richly coloured painting.
Literature: Noh dramas by Kannami (1333–84) and his son Zeami (1363–1443). Kyogen (comic interludes) performed with Noh plays. Emergence of Renga (linked verse), by poets such as Sogi (1421–1502), leading to Haiku (3 line poems).
Tea Ceremony: Rules laid down by Sen no Rikyu (1521–91).

AZUCHI-MOMOYAMA PERIOD (1568–1615)
Architecture: New type of castle architecture: Shirasagi (White Heron) castle in Himeji. Development of tea house, Chashitsu.
Painting: Gold leaf screen and wall paintings by Hasegawa Tohaku and Kano Eitoku (1543–90). Namban screens, depicting foreigners.

EDO OR TOKUGAWA PERIOD
Sculpture: Polychrome carvings of Nikko shrines. Genroku culture (1688-1703) urban merchant phenomenon.
Painting: Colour wood-block prints or Ukiyo-e, depicting urban pleasure quarters and, later, landscapes. Principal artists: Harunobu, Kiyonobu (1664–1729), Utamaro (1753–1806), Sharaku (c.1790), Hokusai (1760–1849), Hiroshige (1797–1858).
Ogata Koetsu produced paintings, designs, lacquers, and pottery. Development of naturalistic and anti-naturalistic schools of art. Western art also begins to influence Japan, notably the work of Ikeno Taiga and Watanabe Kazan.
Literature: Matsuo Bashō (1644–94), greatest master of the haiku. Other important poets and haiku writers: Yosa Buson and Kobayashi Issa. Novels change to suit the growing merchant class, e.g. *Five Women who Loved Love*. The puppet theatre (jōruri) develops. Kabuki dramas with live actors.

MEIJI AND MODERN PERIODS
(after 1868)
Influence of Western literature. Yosano, Akiko (1878–1942) woman poet of great emotional power. Hagiwara, Sakutarō (1888–1942) first major poet to write in colloquial Japanese. Ishikawa, Takuboku (1885–1912) popular modern *waka* poet. First modern Japanese novel by Futabatei, Shimei (1864–1909), *The Drifting Cloud*. *Rashomōn*, by Akutagawa, Ryūnosuke (1892–1927) achieved considerable renown. *The Dancing Girl of Izu*, by Kawabata, Yasunari (1899–1972), psychological novel. *Twilight Crane*, a play by Kinoshita, Junji (1914–) uses old folklore for modern drama.

HOW TO PRONOUNCE THE JAPANESE WORDS IN THIS BOOK
"a" as in are
"e" as in when
"i" as in it
"o" as in not
"o" as in oh
"u" as in put
"ai" as in 'y' of my
"ei" as in 'ay' of day
Other vowels, if together, are pronounced separately, e.g. Ieyasu (I-e-ya-s-u). Consonants are pronounced as in English, except that "g" is mostly hard as in "go", never soft as in "gentry". Most syllables are evenly stressed, as in French.
Samurai (sa-mu-rai): member of warrior class
Shogun (Sho-o-gun) military ruler. (Sometimes, as in "Shogun" the vowel sound is doubled.)
Hana (Ha-na): flower
Basho (Ba-sho-o): banana tree
"u" is often silent. Sukiyaki sounds like Skiyaki.

JAPANESE NAMES
In Japan the family name is put first, and then the personal name, e.g. Minamoto Yoritomo. Minamoto is the clan name; Yoritomo is the *shogun's* personal name. Tokugawa Ieyasu is the correct order to the Japanese eye and ear. "Ieyasu Tokugawa" would sound as odd to the Japanese as "Churchill Winston" would to us.
    Many feminine personal names have the suffix "ko" which is written with the character for "child". e.g. Hanako: Flower-child, and Yuriko: Lily-child. Many surnames describe the places at which people's ancestors lived, e.g. Matsushita (Ma-tsushta) means beneath the pine trees. Tanaka means amid the rice fields.

Reference
The Economy

Facts and figures
GNP: (1971) 79 trillion yen, showing annual growth rate of 15% over 10 years (second in non-communist world).
Per capita income: 613.5 thousand yen (20th in world).
Main sources of income:
Agriculture: Rice, wheat, barley, livestock, fruit, vegetables.
Forestry: Nearly 70% of land area. Coniferous and broadleaved. 2.1 billion cubic metres of wood. Building material and paper.
Fishing: Frozen and canned fish, especially tuna and crabmeat, whaling products; pearls.
Industry: Iron and steel, electrical machinery, electronics, shipbuilding, motor vehicles, aircraft, precision instruments, chemicals, textiles, paper, ceramics.
Main trading partners: United States (biggest single partner), Canada, Asia, Europe, Australia.
Currency: Yen. Notes from 100 yen to 10,000 yen account for 94.4% of currency value. Coins from 1 to 100 yen.
Budget: 1973 revenue 261,682,000 million yen; expenditure 234,464,000 million yen. 1972 expenditure: grants to local government 19%, public works 19%, social security 14%, culture, education and science 12%, defence 7%.

Agriculture in Japan

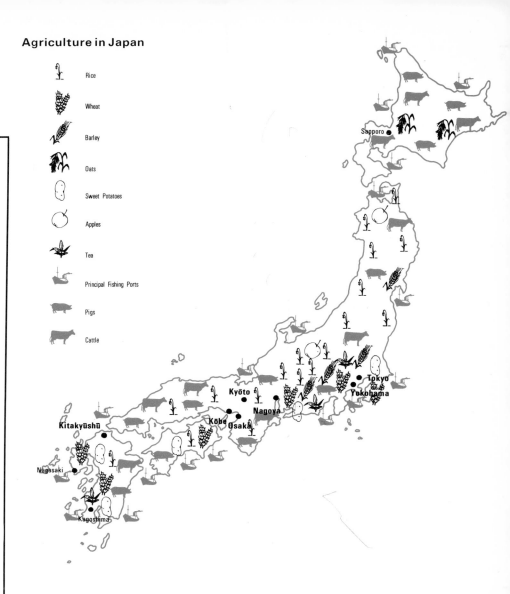

Rice
Wheat
Barley
Oats
Sweet Potatoes
Apples
Tea
Principal Fishing Ports
Pigs
Cattle

The economy after World War Two

Recovery was phenomenally fast. With assistance from the United States, the economy overtook its prewar level in ten years and continued to expand two or three times as fast as that of other industrial nations. Today Japan is the world leader in the production of ships and radios, second in automobiles, television sets and rubber products, and third in cement, iron and steel.

Exports have risen at an average yearly rate of 16.5 per cent in ten years, almost double the average growth rate of world trade. Early in the fifties, light industrial products still accounted for about half of Japan's export value. Now, heavy and chemical industrial products are the most important exports. Imports have also increased steadily. After the war, food and machinery were the chief imports. Today, raw materials make up 70 per cent of imports.

Japanese imports and exports

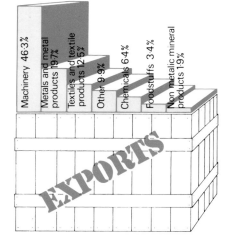

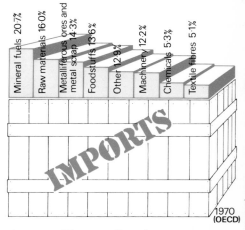

Exports: Machinery 46.3%, Metals and metal products 19.7%, Textiles and textile products 12.5%, Other 9.9%, Chemicals 6.4%, Foodstuffs 3.4%, Non metallic mineral products 1.9%

Imports: Mineral fuels 20.7%, Raw materials 16.0%, Metalliferous ores and metal scrap 14.3%, Foodstuffs 13.6%, Other 12.9%, Machinery 12.2%, Chemicals 5.3%, Textile fibres 5.1%

1970 (OECD)

Japan is essentially a processing nation. Nearly all exports are manufactured goods. A large proportion of imports are raw materials, fuel and food. Japan imports all her supplies of raw cotton, wool and rubber, up to 99% of her supply of crude oil, 96% of her iron ore and more than 60% of her wheat.

Employment in Japan

Employed population 51,992,000

Agriculture, Forestry and Fishing 7,538,840

Manufacturing and Construction 18,145,210

Clerical, Administrative, Civil and Military Services 26,307,950

Non working population 55,208,000

From mass unemployment after the war, Japan now has a labour shortage. This is due to the post-war decline in the birth rate and the growing number of school leavers entering university or college before starting work.

Industry in Japan

🏭	Major Industrial Centres
⚙	Mechanical Engineering
🚗	Automobiles
⛴	Shipbuilding
◎	Rubber
⊡	Electrical Machinery
🍷	Glass
☕	Ceramics
⊓	Cement
▱	Paper

Textiles

Principal Coalmining Areas

Iron-metallurgy

Oil Refineries

Chemicals

Sapporo

Tokyo
Yokohama
Kyōto
Nagoya
Kōbe
Osaka
Kitakyūshū
Nagasaki
Kagoshima

The goods owned by Japanese people

Living standards throughout Japan are fairly uniform. There are few very poor people. Most households have a television set, a washing machine, a refrigerator and a vacuum cleaner.

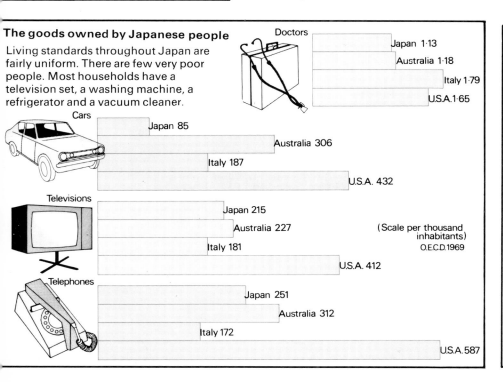

Doctors
Japan 1·13
Australia 1·18
Italy 1·79
U.S.A. 1·65

Cars
Japan 85
Australia 306
Italy 187
U.S.A. 432

Televisions
Japan 215
Australia 227
Italy 181
U.S.A. 412

(Scale per thousand inhabitants)
O.E.C.D. 1969

Telephones
Japan 251
Australia 312
Italy 172
U.S.A. 587

The rise in prices and incomes

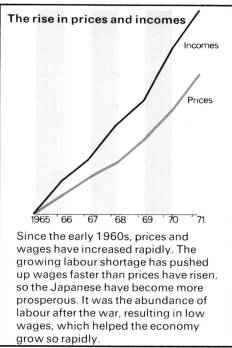

Incomes

Prices

1965 66 67 68 69 70 71

Since the early 1960s, prices and wages have increased rapidly. The growing labour shortage has pushed up wages faster than prices have risen, so the Japanese have become more prosperous. It was the abundance of labour after the war, resulting in low wages, which helped the economy grow so rapidly.

Gazetteer

Japan has four main islands: **Hokkaido**, **Honshu**, **Kyushu**, and **Shikoku**. The name of the island on which a town is situated, is given just after the name of the town.

Akita, Honshu (39 45N 140 6E) Pop. (1965) 216,606 Port. Exports petroleum.

Asahikawa, Hokkaido (43 50N 142 20E) Pop. (1965) 245,243. Brewing of *sake*; manufactures wood products and textiles.

Chiba, Honshu (35 40N 140 6E) Pop. (1965) 332,174. Manufactures steel, paper, textiles.

Fujiyama (Mount Fuji) (35 30N 139 0E) Japan's highest mountain; on Honshu Is. A volcanic crater, 3,776 metres (12,395 ft) high. Last eruption in 1707. Sacred in Shinto religion, and famous for its beauty.

Fukuoka, Kyushu (33 36N 130 27E) Cap. of Fukuoka Pref. Pop. (1965) 749,808. Exports porcelain and machinery. Manufactures textiles, chemicals, pottery, metal products. Imperial University of Kyushu 1910.

Gifu, Honshu (35 30N 136 54E) Cap. of Gifu Pref. Pop. (1965) 358,130. Light industry: parasols, fans, lanterns, textiles, cutlery. Fishing centre. Tourist resort.

Hamamatsu, Honshu (34 45N 137 50E) Pop. (1965) 392,632. Manufactures motor cycles, pianos, organs, chemicals, cloth.

Himeji, Honshu (34 56N 134 48E) Pop. (1965) 367,798. Manufactures textiles, chemicals, leather products.

Hiroshima, Honshu (34 30N 132 35E) Cap. of Hiroshima Pref. Pop. (1965) 504,227. Seaport and industrial centre. Shipbuilding, brewing. Manufactures motor vehicles, machinery, rubber, textiles. On August 6, 1945, the first atomic bomb used in warfare was dropped here; the city was destroyed and 160,000 people were killed or severely wounded. The city has been rebuilt.

Hokkaido Island (43 30N 143 0E) Most northerly of the four main islands, and very mountainous. Separated from Honshu by the Tsugaru Strait. Pop. (1965) 5,039,206. The coldest island; parts are foggy. Heavily forested. Coalfields, fishing, forestry, agriculture. Most of Japan's Ainu (about 15,000 people) live on Hokkaido. Settled on by Japanese in the 16th century.

Honshu Island (36N 139E) Largest and most important of the four main islands. Pop. (1960) 71,354,357. Includes 34 of Japan's 46 prefectures. Contains most of the important towns. Separated from Hokkaido by the Tsugaru Strait, from Shikoku by the Kii Channel, from Kyushu by the Bungo Channel.

Kagoshima, Kyushu (31 48N 130 40E) Cap. of Kagoshima Pref. Pop. (1965) 328,444. Minor seaport near the volcano Sakurajima. Manufactures textiles and metal goods.

Kanazawa, Honshu (35 25N 139 20E) Cap. of Ishikawa Pref. Pop. (1965) 335,825. Manufactures textiles, machinery, porcelain, lacquerware. Famous for landscape gardening.

Kawasaki, Honshu (35 4N 139 35E) Pop. (1965) 854,776. Shipbuilding, engineering. Manufactures steel and textiles.

Kitakyushu, Kyushu (33 52N 130 45E). City formed in 1963 by union of Mojii, Kokura, Tobata, Yawata, Wakamatsu. Pop. (1965) 1,042,389. Industrial, Kyushu Institute of Technology founded 1909.

Kobe, Honshu (34 45N 135 12E) Cap. of Hyogo Pref. Pop. (1965) 1,216,579. Seaport stretching nine miles along the coast of Osaka Bay. Exports ships, metal goods, textiles. Shipbuilding industry. Manufactures chemicals, textiles, rubber. Sugar-milling. Severely damaged during 2nd World War: much of it rebuilt.

Kumamoto, Kyushu (32 40N 130 45E) Cap. of Kumamoto Pref. Pop. (1965) 407,047. Food-processing. Manufactures textiles. Medical University 1949. 16th century castle.

Kyoto, Honshu (35 0N 135 30E) Cap. of Kyoto Pref. Pop. (1965) 1,364,977. Famous for its crafts: porcelain, lacquer work, dolls, fans, silk goods, brocades. Manufactures machinery, textiles, chemicals. Centre of Buddhist religion. Many fine temples, and a former imperial palace. Important tourist centre. University 1897. Kyoto is renowned for its beauty.

Kyushu Island (32 30N 131 0E) Southernmost of the four main islands. Pop. (1960) 12,903,515. Mountainous and has a volcano on Mt. Aso. Hot springs.

Nagasaki, Kyushu (32 40N 129 48E) Cap. of Nagasaki Pref. Pop. (1965) 405,479. Seaport. Exports coal, cement, tinned fish. Shipbuilding, engineering. It was the only Japanese port open to foreign trade in the 16th century. August 9, 1945, the second atomic bomb ruined the city, and 26,000 were killed, 40,000 injured.

Nagoya, Honshu (35 17N 137 0E) Cap. of Aichi Pref. Pop. (1965) 1,935,430. Seaport, and Japan's 3rd largest city. Opened to foreign trade in 1907. Manufactures machinery, porcelain, textiles, chemicals. University 1939. 17th century castle damaged in the 2nd World War. Buddhist temple of Higashi Honganji.

Naha, on Okinawa Island (26 10N 127 45E) Pop. (1960) 250,832. Seaport, and largest city on S.W. coast. Headquarters of the U.S. military, and seat of local government of the Ryukyu Islands. Exports sugar, dried fish. Manufactures textiles, pottery.

Niigata, Honshu (38 0N 139 5E) Cap. of Niigata Pref. Pop. (1965) 356,302. Chief seaport on W. coast of Honshu. The harbour is unsheltered and tends to silt up. Niigata exports oil, fertilizers. Manufactures chemicals, machinery, textiles.

Okayama, Honshu (34 40N 133 6E) Cap. of Okayama Pref. Pop. (1965) 291,816). Port. Manufactures agricultural implements, cotton goods, porcelain.

Okinawa Island (26 30N 128 0E) Largest of the Ryukyu Islands. Area 454 sq.m. Pop. (1956) 758,777. Sugar-cane; sweet potatoes, rice. American military base. During the 2nd World War, there was fierce fighting on Okinawa between Japanese and American troops.

Osaka, Honshu (34 40N 135 39E) Cap. Osaka Pref. Pop. (1965) 3,156,201. Seapo[rt] Exports textiles, machinery, metal goo[ds]. Manufactures steel, chemicals, cement. Ma[ny] cotton mills: called "The Manchester [of] Japan". University 1931. 16th century cast[le.] Many Buddhist and Shinto temples. Heav[ily] bombed in 2nd World War.

Ryukyu Islands (26 30N 128 0E) Arch[i]pelago between Kyushu and Taiwan, in [a] chain 700m. long. Pop. (1963) 908,00[0] Some of the islands are volcanic. Swe[et] potatoes, sugar-cane. The chief island [is] Okinawa; chief town, Naha. Japanese sin[ce] 1879. Under American control since 194[?]. In 1953 the northern Amami-Oshima Gro[up] was restored to Japan.

Sapporo, Hokkaido (43 1N 141 15E) Ca[p.] of Sapporo Pref. Pop. (1965) 794,90[0] Flour-milling, brewing, sawmilling. Man[u]factures agricultural machinery. Hokkaid[o] University 1918.

Sendai, Honshu (38 15N 141 0E) Cap. [of] Miyagi Pref. Pop. (1965) 481,013. Foo[d-] processing. Manufactures metal goods, te[x]tiles, pottery. Tohoku University 1907.

Shikoku Island (33 30N 133 30E) Smalle[st] of the four main islands. Mountainous a[nd] thickly forested; Rice, tobacco, soya bea[ns] in lowlands.

Shizuoka, Honshu (34 59N 138 30E) Ca[p.] of Shizuoka Pref. Pop. (1965) 367,705. [A] tea-growing region. Tea-processing a[nd] packing. Trade in oranges. Manufactur[es] machinery, chemicals. University 1949.

Tokyo, Honshu (35 48N 139 45E) Cap. [of] Japan. World's most populous city. Po[p.] (1965) 10,348,975. Seaport for coastal shi[p]ping. Port amalgamated with Yokohama [in] 1941, as Keihin. Shipbuilding, engineerin[g,] printing, publishing. Manufactures textile[s,] chemicals, cars. Shiba Park and Ueno Pa[rk.] Four Universities, 1875, 1877, 1946, 194[9.] Institute of Technology, 1881. Tokyo w[as] founded as Edo, or Yedo, in the late 12[th] century. Capital since 1868. Great Earthqua[ke] and Fire in 1923. Severe damage during t[he] 2nd World War.

Toyama, Honshu (36 40N 137 10E) Cap. [of] Toyama Pref. Pop. (1965) 239,809. Man[u]factures patent medicines and drugs, textile[s,] chemicals, machinery.

Wakayama, Honshu (34 10N 135 12E) Ca[p.] of Wakayama Pref. Pop. (1965) 328,64[?] Manufactures iron, steel, textiles, chemica[ls,] sake.

Yokohama (35 25N 139 35E) Cap. [of] Yokohama Pref., on W. shore of Tokyo Ba[y.] Pop. (1965) 1,788,796. Japan's 4th large[st] city. Seaport handling about one third [of] foreign trade. Exports silk, rayon, canned fis[h.] Manufactures steel, motor vehicles, chem[i]cals. Shipbuilding. Oil-refining. First po[rt] open to foreign trade, in 1859. Great Eart[h]quake, 1923. Severe damage in 2nd Wor[ld] War.

Yokosuka (35 18N 139 36E) Seaport a[nd] naval base on S.W. coast of Tokyo Bay. [Pop.] (1965) 317,410. Shipbuilding.

Index

Numbers in **heavy** type refer to illustrations.

Actors; of female parts 30
Advertising **29**
Ainu 8, **9**
America 12, **13**, 22, 32, **44**, 46, 53
Annual festivals **20, 21**, 51
Arable land 32
Archery 19
Architecture 8, 30, **31**
Artisans, in Tokugawa class system, **43**
Arts, Japanese influence on 12, **13**
Asahi Shimbun **29**
Asakusa district, Tokyo **10**
Asano Naganori 48, **49**
Atomic bomb 12, **46**

Baseball 18, **18**
Bashō 30
Baths 14, **36**
Beaches 21
Beans 25
Beauty, of Japan **11**, 20
Beauty, Japanese concept of 30
Beds, Japanese style 14
Bento (picnic box) 27
Bon festival 36
Boxer Rising, China, 1900, **45**
Boys' festival 37
Buddha, Todaiji image of **39**
Buddhism 8, 10, 26, 30, **30, 31**, 36, **37**, 38, **39**, 48, **48**
Bullet train 34, **35**
Business companies 32, 51

Calligraphy 16, **28**, 28
Car industry 33
Carp streamers 37
Chambara (sword-clash) **29**
Chanoyu (tea ceremony) **50**
Charter Oath of Five Articles, 1868 **45**
Cherry blossom 16
China 8, **8**, 30, 31, 38, **44**
Chopsticks 26, **27**
Christianity 38, **39**, 42
Chrysanthemum leaves 27
Class divisions, under Tokugawa shogunate **43**, 44
Coffee houses 16, 28
Colonial expansion 46
Confucianism **43**
Conscription, military 44, **45**
Constitution, of 1889 44
Craft shops 25

Daimyo (feudal landowners) 42, **42, 43**
Datsun cars 10
Department stores 24, **24**
Drama 30, **31**
Dried snakes, medicinal **25**
"Dubbing" in films **29**

Edo (old name of Tokyo) 40, 42, **43**, 48
Educational system 22, **22**
Eggs 26, **26, 27**
Emperor, divinity of 38, 47
Employment 23, **32**
"Exam hell" 23
Expo '70, Osaka 47

Farming **32**
Feudal Period 8
Films, Japanese **13**, 29
First World War 45
Fish farms 33
Fishing **11**, 33, **52**
Flats 14, **14**
Food 24, **24**, 25, 26, **26, 27**
Footgear, inside house 14, **36**
Forty-Seven Ronin 48, **49**
French Impressionists **13**
Fujiwara family 8, **9**
Funerals **37**
Furoshiki (carrying-cloth) 24

Gagaku (courtly music) **31**
Garden, raked 30
Geisha **10**, 16, **17**
Genji, Prince 48

Haniwa figures 8
Hawaii, for holidays 20
Heian Period 8
Heiji Monogatari **9**
Hirohito 46, **46, 47**
Hiroshige 43
Hiroshima 12, **46**
Hokkaido 10
Hokusai 31
Holidays **20**, 20, **21**
Horyuji Temple 8
Hot-spring resorts 20
House, Japanese **14**
Hovercraft **35**
Hydro-electrical power **11**

Ideographs 28
Ikebana (flower arrangement) **17**
Imperial line 8
Industrial production 12
Industrialization 32, 33, **45**
Iron imports 32
Isolation policy 10, 42

Japanese International Air Lines **34**
Jimmu Tenno 8
Jodo Buddhism 38
Jomon culture 8
Judo 12, **19**

Kabuki theatre 30, **49**
Kakure-Krishitan (secret Christians) 38
Kami 38, **50**
Kannushi (Shinto priest) 38
Kanto earthquake, 1923 40, **40**, 46
Karate **19**
Kato, Olympic champion 18
Kendo **19**
Kindergarten **22**
Kobe 18, 34, **34**
Korea 12, **13**, 31

Koto **31**
Koya monastery 48
"Knock-down" cars 33
Kurosawa, Akira **13**, 31
Kyogashi (sweetmeats) 27
Kyoto 8, **8**, 10, **10**, 31, 40, **51**

Landscape gardening **10**, 30
Language, Japanese 28
Learning by rote 23
Loyalty 48, 50

Magnificent Seven, The **13**
Mainichi Shimbun **29**
Management and workers **13**
Manchuria 12, **45**, 46
Markets, local 24, **25**
Mathematics 23
Matsushita electronics **10**
Meat 24, 26, **26**
Meiji ("Enlightened Rule") **44**, 44, **45**, 49
Merchants, in Tokugawa class system **43**
Merchant fleet, Japanese **35**
"Mongolian" type 8, **9**
Mountains 10, **11**, 16, 20
Murasaki Shikibu 48

Nagasaki 42
Nagoya 34, **34**
Nanzenji, Zen Temple **10**
Nara 8, **10**, 20, **39**, 40
Natural objects, worship of 36
New Year 36, **40**
Newspapers 28, **29**
Nikon cameras **10**
Nirvana **39**
Noh theatre 30, **31**

Oda Nobunaga 42, **42**
Okinawa 46
Olympic Games, 1964 34
Olympic Games, 1972 18
On 50
Osaka 34, **47**
Osaka Castle 42

Pachinko (pinball) 15
Painting **13**, 28
Paper, hand-made 33
Pearl Harbour 12, **13**, 46
Pearl industry 33
Peasants, in Tokugawa class system **43**, 49
Peking, Siege of 45
Perry, Matthew 44, **44**
Pilgrimages 20
Poems 28, 30
Pollution 52, **52**
Pottery 8, 32
Prints, wood-blocks **13**, **28**

Railways 34
Rice 8, 24, 26, **26, 27**, 32
Rice paper **28**
Roads 34, **34**
Roman letters (Romaji) **29**
Rush hour, in Tokyo **11, 35**
Russia 10, 44, **45**, 46, **47**
Ryokan (inns) 20, **21**

Sabi, sabishisa 30
Saigo Takamori, **49**
Sake (rice wine) 26

Samurai 19, **29**, 31, **43**, 44, **45, 49**
Sashimi (sliced raw fish) 27
Satsuma rebels 44
School uniform, national 23
Seafood **25**, 26, **26**
Seal, for identification 28
Second World War 12, **13**, 22, **33**, 40
Sen-gakuji Temple, Tokyo 48
Sesshu 30
Seven Samurai, The 13
Shingon Buddhism 48
Shinjuku **41**
Shinshu Buddhism 38
Shinto **25**, 36, **36**, 38, **38, 39**
Shipbuilding **10**, 53
Shogunate 42
Shops, neighbourhood 24, **25**
Shotoku Taishi 8
Shrines, Shinto 38
Singapore, capture of 12
Snakes **36**
Sokka Gakkai **39**
Soya bean 26, **26, 27**
"Spring struggle" **52**
Steel technology, Japanese 32
Suicide **51**
Sukiyaki 26, **27**
Sumo wrestling 16, 18, **18**
Suzuki Harunobu **13**

Taira family **9**
Tatami 14, **25, 33**
Tea 26, **26**, 27
Television ("Terebi") 16, 28, **29, 33**
Tempura (food fried in batter) **27**
Tenrikyo **39**
Thailand **13**
Todaiji Temple, Nara **39**
Tojo, General 46
Tokaido Line 34
Tokaido road **43**
Tokugawa shogunate 40, 42, **42, 43**, 44
Tokugawa Ieyasu 42, **42, 43**
Tokyo **10, 11, 16**, 23, **29**, 34, **35, 40, 41**, 46, **48, 52**
Tokyo tower 40
Tomb culture 8
Torii 38
Tsushima, Battle of 10
Typewriter, Japanese 28

University 22, **22**, 23
Utagaruta (card game) **37**

Winter sports 20, **21**

Xavier, Francis 38

Yamoto area 8
Yayoi period 8
Yen 24
"Yojimbo" ("The Hired Man") **31**
Yokohama 34
Yomiuri Shimbun **29**
Yokozuma (Sumo Grand Champion) 18

Zen Buddhism **10**, 30, 38, **50**

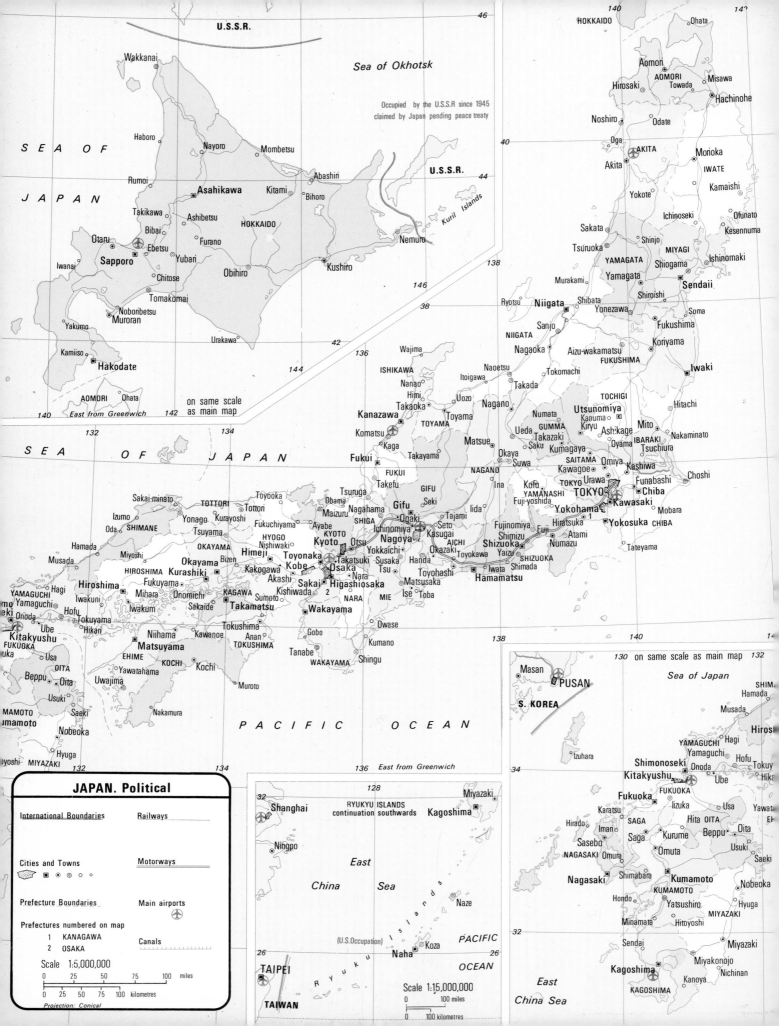